THE ABDUCTION OF A LIMERICK HEIRESS:
*Social and political relations in
mid-eighteenth-century Ireland*

Maynooth Studies in Local History

GENERAL EDITOR   Raymond Gillespie

This is one of six new pamphlets published in 1998 in the Maynooth Studies in Local History series. Like their fourteen predecessors these volumes illustrate, through case studies of particular areas and themes, how life in Ireland in the past evolved in a variety of settings, both urban and rural. As such they join a rapidly growing literature dealing with the local dimension of Ireland's past. That 'localness' is not primarily territorial, although all are firmly rooted in a sense of place, but derives from an awareness of the regional diversity of Irish society in the past.

Local history is not about administrative frameworks or geographical entities but rather about the people who created the social worlds which made particular places distinctive. These pamphlets are therefore primarily about people who lived in particular places over time. The range of people explored is wide; from the poor of pre-famine Drogheda and Ferbane through the nouveau riche world of the Meath grazier to the aristocratic lifestyle of an eighteenth-century Tipperary landlord. What all these people have in common is that they shaped their particular places in response to stimuli both from within their communities and from the wider world.

Like their predecessors these pamphlets allow us a brief glimpse into the diverse, interacting worlds which are the basis of the Irish historical experience. In their own right they are each significant contributions to our understanding of that experience in all its richness and complexity. They present local history as the vibrant and challenging discipline that it is.

Maynooth Studies in Local History: Number 20

The Abduction of a Limerick Heiress:

Social and political relations in mid-eighteenth-century Ireland

Toby Barnard

IRISH ACADEMIC PRESS

First published in 1998 by
IRISH ACADEMIC PRESS
44, Northumberland Road, Dublin 4, Ireland
and in North America by
IRISH ACADEMIC PRESS
c/o ISBS, 5804 NE Hassalo Street, Portland, OR 97213
website: http://www.iap.ie

British Library Cataloguing in Publication Data

Barnard, Toby
    The abduction of a Limerick heiress: social and political
    relations in mid-eighteenth century Ireland. – (Maynooth
    studies in local history)
    1. Abduction – Ireland – Limerick – History – 18th century
    2. Inheritance and succession – Ireland – History – 18th
    century 3. Ireland – Social conditions – 18th century
    4. Ireland – Social life and customs – 18th century
    I. Title
    941.9'45

    ISBN 0716527154

Typeset in 10 pt on 12 pt Bembo by
Carrigboy Typesetting Services, County Cork
Printed by ColourBooks Ltd., Dublin

Contents

Preface

I am delighted, having been associated with the M.A. in local history at Maynooth virtually from its inception, to contribute this study to the accompanying series of publications. Serendipity otherwise explains the origins of this project. Chancing on a copy of S.R. Penny's *Smythe of Barbavilla* in a second-hand bookshop in Oxford alerted me to the possible survival of an archive. Soon I discovered it was located, like so much else important to the history of Ireland, in the nether reaches of the National Library of Ireland. Without the labours and kindness of Catherine Fahy and Tom Desmond this account could never have been attempted. Subsequently I learnt that Desmond FitzGerald, the Knight of Glin, had earlier worked through this collection and appreciated its potential. He greatly encouraged me to undertake this study. He showed me sites, tracked down portraits and, with Olda, baited me during my Limerick rambles. Through him I also met Topper and Hilary White at Nantenan, Hugh Massy at Stoneville and Robert Guinness at Park Lodge, all of whom have interested themselves in what I was doing. An invitation from Bernadette Whelan and John Logan to speak at the University of Limerick obliged me to set my thoughts in order. In addition this occasion brought me into contact with Peggy Barry, Liam Irwin, Patrick O'Connor and Chris O'Mahony, who enabled me to add much local detail. Later Austin Bouvenizer kindly allowed me to read the Brown-Southwell manuscripts at Rathkeale. My good friend, Derry Falvey, took me twice to view Massy Lodge. The Hanleys generously permitted us to inspect this fascinating house.

In ways that they may not always recognise (or even like) I have benefited from the conversations and writings – some as yet unpublished – of Danny Beaumont, Sean Connolly, Arch Elias, Neal Garnham, David Hayton, Jimmy Kelly, Mary-Lou Legg and Anthony O'Connor. What I owe to Valerie Kemp for rescuing me from my technological luddism can scarcely be expressed. Much of the research was begun while I was in Dublin thanks to a grant from the Leverhulme Foundation. The writing was finished during the early stages of my tenure of a British Academy research readership. To both institutions I am most grateful; as also to the Harding Research Fund of Hertford College (and its coordinator) for financing other parts of the archival work. Over the years I have gained much from my links with the history department at Maynooth. In its adjunct, the research institute in Drumcondra, I have been welcomed, assisted and stimulated by Bernadette Cunningham and Raymond Gillespie. Thus, I too have enjoyed the inspirational guidance which so many of the M.A. students receive.

Abductions

In May 1744 excited correspondents reported how a wealthy young woman had been accorded a *joyeuese entrée* into the city of Limerick. Attended by three servants – one of them exotically a blackamoor – and with caparisoned horses, the visitor was mobbed by a 'multitude' keen to behold her. The cathedral bells rang out to greet her arrival, and a barrel of beer refreshed the throng.[1] This celebrity acclaimed like Baba, the bearded Turkish woman in *The Rake's Progress*, was Frances Ingoldsby. With her sister she had inherited an estate centred on Limerick: her own share was valued at an annual £870.[2] She was not, however, welcomed primarily as a returning landowner. Instead the ostentatious courtesies announced support for one side in a contest which revealed and, in its turn, worsened divisions within the locality. Moreover, the demonstrations merely marked a stage in a protracted struggle which spluttered on beyond 1780.

The protagonists who ranged themselves either behind or against Frances Ingoldsby and Hugh Fitzjohn Massy, her abductor and new husband, tell something of the fissures among the propertied of Limerick and its environs. By looking harder at the groups which now confronted each other it is possible to gauge the continuing importance of familial and territorial affinities in the public life of Protestant Ireland during the eighteenth century.

Such an investigation also encourages speculation about the relative weight in such configurations of kinship, neighbourhood, ethnicity, confession and even ideology. Furthermore, because this episode was played out – for the most part – in the provinces, it prompts reflections on how local and apparently trivial disputes connected with and influenced the politics of Dublin Castle and College Green. A more inclusive view of politics, to encompass the seemingly bizarre and trivial such as Frances Ingoldsby's abduction, will be offered.

The central act in the drama, the removal of Frances Ingoldsby from a country rectory in County Limerick after dusk on a Sunday evening in November 1743, is an example of an activity familiar in characterizations of eighteenth-century Ireland. Abductions, sometimes individually or – more often – collectively, have long been felt to tell of the malaise of Irish society. The nineteenth-century historian, J.A. Froude, argued that abductions betrayed the sectarian animosity of dispossessed Catholics towards the newly ascendant Protestants.[3] However, Froude's reading was almost immediately questioned by W.E.H. Lecky. The latter treated the activity as an element in the economic backwardness and cultural primitivism for which he belaboured newcomers and natives alike.[4] Undoubtedly the persistence of abductions, together with the responses of spectators as well as actors, betrayed an ambivalent attitude among many members of the Protestant elite towards the law and its enforcement. Even at the time, and certainly since, the repercussions from such violence stimulated disquiet about the position of women within eighteenth-century Ireland.[5] The phenomenon of abduction has recently been placed on a more secure foundation thanks to a careful statistical analysis. As a result precision has replaced the earlier speculations. By analysing the cases reported in the newspapers, Dr. James Kelly has shown how, usually, they involved Protestants both as instigators and victims.[6] Social and economic factors of the kind favoured by Lecky are not discarded. The miscreants often inhabited the margins of landed society. As cadets with meagre inheritances they were obliged to support their pretensions to an inherited gentility by means other than those of the leisured landowner. Too often their regular revenues could not buy the style of life to which they aspired. Supplements were accordingly sought. The carrying off of young women of fortune smacked of a remote and backward world. Yet, frequently successful, it constituted a rational way to supplement puny assets. Furthermore, Dr. Kelly's researches have shown that this form of violence was not concentrated in the most inaccessible and under-developed part of the kingdom. Dublin saw the most. Outside the capital, the behaviour persisted longest in Counties Cork, Kilkenny, Limerick and Tipperary. These were regions undergoing rapid, although uneven, economic and cultural transformations as commercialization challenged custom.[7]

What was at stake when a young woman was snatched was property. With possession of an heiress (even to a modest inheritance) came the prospect of commanding her goods. The violence simply truncated or circumvented the more orthodox but cumbersome rituals of courtship and negotiation. Such direct methods had been favoured in both medieval Ireland and England. Stringent statutes against abduction were passed by the Dublin parliament.[8] Yet at the same time as members of parliament tightened the provisions of these laws, they connived at, even occasionally participated in, the crime. If responses varied, so did what was involved in the abductions. At worst, an abductor might kill his victim, as happened when John McNaghten attempted to seize Mary Anne Knox in County Londonderry in 1761. NcNaghten was apprehended by the military and subsequently hanged.[9] Sometimes captive knew captor, so much so that the girl could be suspected of colluding in her own removal. In such cases abduction looked like, and would be treated as, a brusque device to expedite a marriage treaty which might otherwise be wearisomely prolonged. Boldness did pay off: the resulting matches were accepted as legal. This indeed was the outcome of Massy's seizure of Frances Ingoldsby. Once Massy was decreed to be her husband, he gained undisputed control of her body and property. But he did so only after an angry struggle during which he was brought before the law courts. The guardians of Frances Ingoldsby were affluent and powerful. As makers and enforcers of the law it was hardly surprising that they turned to it for remedy. In this instance, as in many others where the result is known, statute and proclamation failed to retrieve the abducted heiress. The high probability of an abductor being left to enjoy his prize encouraged direct action. It also throws into doubt the ability of the law to police unruly quarters of eighteenth-century Ireland.

Those women lucky enough to be prised away from their abductors and returned to their relations did not always consider themselves as fortunate. Thereafter the victim was regarded as indelibly sullied, and her value in any marriage market much reduced. This was so widely appreciated that the law tended to be invoked more to pursue and harass the malefactors than to recover the victim. Frances Ingoldsby would eventually be ceded to her captors, in part because her erstwhile protectors lost interest in keeping her. Her reputation, like that of so many others caught up in such episodes, was blemished. A double standard, in which women were judged more severely than men, operated.[10] It is unclear how much the men who perpetrated such violence were damaged. A contemporary scandal across the border from Limerick in County Cork suggested the prevalent complaisance. A modest landowner of standing comparable to Massy, Will Crofts, was embroiled in a forced marriage. At first the young squireen was condemned by his neighbours for having misled a weaker companion. But soon enough the hasty alliance was accepted. The incident intensified existing animosities rather than created new ones. Crofts, although of a family settled in the north Cork barony for at least a century, was reviled by a local magistrate, who expostulated, 'how dare such a fellow as I talk to him, one who sprung from jockeys, grooms and coachmen'.[11] Censorious neighbours had doubted how industrious a tenant farmer Crofts would prove to be. Worries about him lingered: 'such are his vanity and inclinations to expense and appearances that he will not improve his fortune'.[12] To the hostile, then, Crofts possessed traits associated with the supposedly parasitic middlemen, aspiring to the habits of a gentleman without the attendant labour of overseeing and farming the lands which he rented on easy terms.[13] Something of the same circumstances and outlook distinguished Hugh Massy and his comrades. Bagging a local heiress offered an excellent way to ease their pinched condition.

Abductions were not uniform. Degrees of violence, provocation and collusion differed. The distinctive features in each case helped to determine public and private responses. For the consciously civilized and polite, these rough exploits belonged to a boorish world from which they had long since separated and which they were eager to eradicate. Yet even some who prided themselves on their respect for the law and elegant manners might wink at violence. Knowledge of and intimacy with the participants modified theoretical hostility. Attitudes towards what Hugh Fitzjohn Massy had done reflected the complexity of existing relationships within the vicinity. For those already antipathetic to the Massys the abduction confirmed what they had always alleged. It supplied additional ammunition in a lengthy campaign to discredit the Massys as uncouth and aggressive, and so to thwart their further advance. Others already allied by kinship, neighbourhood or interest with the Massys lionized the bravo. Furthermore, the marriage, since it allowed Massy to raid his wife's estate to reward his own followers, tightened the bonds of dependency.

The Ingoldsby chronicle confirms what Froude and Lecky appreciated long ago. Abductions uncover awkward facets of Hanoverian Ireland. Those in authority displayed a disconcerting insouciance towards aspects of the laws which they were charged to uphold and from which they profited. Furthermore, the fickleness of contemporary opinions towards these escapades reminds of the motley materials from which the accounts were fashioned. What did or did not happen to Frances Ingoldsby may in many vital details remain unknown and unknowable. For the most part, what occurred has to be reconstructed from reports overtly hostile to the Massys. These were largely compiled by the local agents of Frances Ingoldsby's guardians; and it is only through the archive of one of them, William Smythe of Barbavilla, that they have survived.[14] In some cases, Smythe's informants told him what he hoped to hear. In others, protracted litigation generated depositions and briefing papers which obey legal conventions or in which adroit attorneys lead witnesses into particular statements. What is conspicuously absent is any explanation or extenuation on the Massys' side. Partial as the evidence is, both directly and unwittingly it affords unexpected insights. These go beyond the incident itself or even the genus to which it belonged. As has been suggested already by Dr. Kelly and others, the brouhaha reveals much about the position and treatment of women. Then, too, relationships and attitudes are uncovered which can be used to refine recent interpretations of Irish Protestant society. Frances Ingoldsby was so obviously treated as a piece of property, as well as a means to acquire it, that it hardly needs to be repeated that abduction was primarily about property, and the power which went with it. In addition, the politics of Ascendancy Ireland have been shown to revolve around the acquisition, defence and enlargement of the property of a privileged minority.[15] Abductions, although unorthodox, indeed by most definitions illegal, were strategies through which property could be gained. As a public activity to which official agencies customarily responded – by proclamations, fresh statutes, indictment, hue and cry or military posses – the crime had a political dimension. But for other reasons it can also be contended that it belonged to politics.

The Massys were steadily encroaching on the power wielded over Limerick by rivals, who included the Ingoldsbys. The competition turned the occasional parliamentary elections and the more frequent municipal ones into ferocious tussles. Landed society was so polarized that the routines of the county were made into the stuff of politics. The identity of the sheriff pricked each year, the composition of the grand jury which he then empanelled and the foreman which it in turn selected, were all battled over. Partisans dragged the seemingly trivial, such as the result of a horse-race, or the exceptional, like the snatching of Frances Ingoldsby, into the fray. County Limerick was not unusual in the intensity of this partisanship. Thanks to the intermittently abundant testimony deposited by the Ingoldsby affair, some of the tactics, values and differences of the competing groupings come into focus. Winning the legal case mattered materially. Once acquitted – as he was – Massy enjoyed his wife's property. Had he lost, he risked execution. The outcome provided a highly visible index of how the contestants stood in relation to the machinery of the state. Victory had symbolic value too. It boosted morale among the Massys and their allies, and could rightly be taken as a happy augury of the electoral successes which they would achieve in later decades. Thus, a more integrated account of mid-eighteenth-century Irish politics might attend to the demonstrations of strength revealed in affrays, grand and petty juries, and assemblies of followers which congregated at the time of the assizes, municipal elections or parliamentary hustings.[16]

Like most Irish counties, Limerick exhibited striking ecological variegation. The eastern baronies had long attracted settlers, but shaded into the terrain and society of Tipperary. A similar blurring occurred along the frontiers with Cork, Kerry and Clare.[17] Several of those implicated in the Ingoldsby imbroglio had interests which extended beyond County Limerick. The strength of the Massys themselves was said to be concentrated in the uplands which straddled Cork and Limerick. Massy, indeed, faced prosecution in the courts of both counties. Others of his kin and company had powerful links with County Clare. Despite the attractions of the fertile basin of the Shannon and its tributaries and a long history of settlement, including planned plantation during the late sixteenth and early seventeenth centuries as part of the Munster venture, the county did not by the eighteenth century have a larger proportion of Protestants than its neighbours. No more than 12 per cent were returned as Protestants in 1731 and 1733.[18] Many of these no doubt lived in the city of Limerick itself. This conurbation introduced further variety and potential tensions. Probably less than 30 per cent of the city's inhabitants were Protestants.[19] Yet in comparison with its hinterland, this made the place – in common with the other walled towns of the island – into a bastion of the Protestant interest. Physical reminders of its function were unusually vivid. Remnants of the walls which had enabled Limerick to defy the English state twice in the seventeenth century still encircled it.[20] A garrison, nominally at over 1,000 men almost one-tenth of the total in Ireland, emphasized the continuing strategic value of the port.[21] Marching daily to Protestant worship, the soldiers cheered edgy Protestants and overawed the Catholic majority.[22] The officers aligned themselves provocatively in both national and local politics, and thereby further divided the city.[23] The cathedral with its clergy, aptly situated on the King's Island in the shadow of the citadel, embodied another element in the Protestant interest. Although less numerous than the military, the clergy nevertheless exerted influence over opinion through their preaching, and, no less than the soldiery, linked the local with national controversies.[24]

The city nightly shut its gates against intruders.[25] Such barriers could hardly stop the entry of trouble-makers. Shops, markets and fairs regularly drew in the country people.[26] Followers of the landed flooded the city at the time of the assizes and sessions. At its quays were unloaded novelties and sedition, which soon spread through the alleys and into the hinterland.[27] The values of the city and the county could not always be sharply distinguished. Nevertheless, a group of civic notables entrenched itself in the municipality.[28] Members of it exerted themselves to save Frances Ingoldsby from Massy. In the ensuing struggle, it became clear that their power, formidable within the city, did not reach much beyond it. In contrast, the Massys, while not lacking urban supporters, drew their main strength from the countryside, and particularly its remoter and hilly regions. Yet, to represent the tussle over possession of Frances Ingoldsby primarily as a contest between town and country would be to mislead. Nevertheless, for reasons explored later, the erstwhile protectors of Frances Ingoldsby depicted themselves as champions of the civilized and orderly ethos of the towns, and emphasized how far the Massys, sunk in a sinister rusticity, diverged from these standards.

In essence, the competition over Frances Massy, although decked out in the fashionable livery of politeness and decorum, activated long-standing antagonisms. The already fractured Protestant interest was further dislocated. The clash over the Ingoldsby girl is better seen, not as an isolated and bizarre incident, but as a skirmish in warfare which stretched back into the Cromwellian era and forward into the later eighteenth century. Protestants had been intruded into the lands of the county and into the government and trade of the corporation during the 1650s.[29] Their ascendancy, challenged and even reversed in the succeeding decades, was completed in the 1690s.[30] The beneficiaries, although united by a common interest in preserving their privileges, quarrelled incessantly among themselves. Sometimes it looked as if the Protestant ascendancy was inherently factious and fissaporous. The roughly equal bestirred themselves to become pre-eminent. Their quarrels made Hanoverian Limerick a lively place. Its ethnic, confessional and occupational mix did not automatically destabilize it. Nor did its rapid increase in size, as it became the location of a textile industry.[31] But in combination, the ingredients proved volatile. In consequence, the apparently innocent rituals of the liturgical and civic year regularly occasioned riots. At holidays, the desire of country dwellers to assert their interests against those of the townspeople ended in bloodshed.[32] Members of the several urban guilds jockeyed for precedence.[33] Freemen strove to preserve their rights against the encroachments of the common council and aldermen.[34] The stirs over the Ingoldsby heiress once again encouraged a few Limerick oligarchs to range themselves against grandees from outside, headed by Southwell, Evans and the Massys. In this way, during a lull between febrile elections, the incident kept alive a powerful partisanship.

Despite the irruption of the unexpected, in the form of the abduction case, elections most frequently allowed rivals to measure up against each other. Elections might also come unexpectedly. Their frequency between 1692 and 1713 deepened incipient fissures. Limerick city was the setting for much of this activity. But, in the poll for the city seats, freemen from outside the walls outnumbered the residents.[35] Also, as in other sizeable towns, the unenfranchized, including the Catholics, could influence the process. Public demonstrations made clear the preferences of those unable to vote.[36] If much in these contests seemed almost accidental and intensely personal, they were not necessarily devoid of an ideological content. Limerick, a principal theatre of Jacobite resistance, constantly reminded, as symbol and concrete example, of the Catholic issue. This furnished a recurring topic of eighteenth-century politics and divided members of the Protestant elite over how best to treat the Catholics. Other questions, such as Protestant dissent or relations with the executive in Dublin and the distant government in England, also separated Protestants. Early in the eighteenth century, these differences over policy and attitude had been accommodated within the distinct denominations of Whig and Tory.[37] After 1714, few in Protestant Ireland admitted to being Tories, with the attendant whiff of Jacobitism and even treason. Divisions tended to express themselves under the older labels of 'court' and 'country'.[38] But, while the precise terms were abandoned, the familial structures around which Irish Toryism had been organized often survived. As we shall see this was so in Limerick, where the old alliance of Ingoldsbys, Smythes and Higgins again came into play during the city elections of 1727. The persistence of such personal connections, akin to the territorial and familial affinities of Gaelic and gaelicized Ireland, prompts further reflections on the structures and dynamics of provincial Protestant politics during the heyday of the Ascendancy. An analysis of how the groupings confronted one another over Miss Ingoldsby, as they did in the parliamentary elections, may assist understanding.

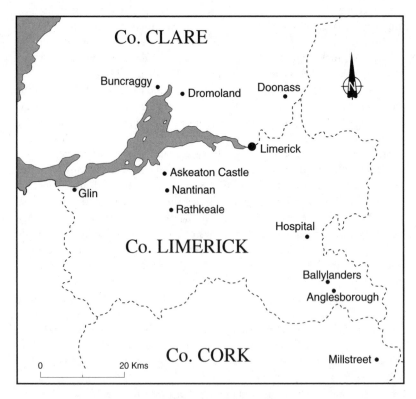

1. Limerick and its environs

Ingoldsbys and Massys

No one disputed the main act in the Limerick drama. After dusk on a Sunday evening in November 1743, Frances Ingoldsby was removed from the parsonage at Nantenan in County Limerick. Thereafter testimonies quickly diverged. It was agreed that force had been used, and that the gang had been armed. But the numbers and circumstances of those involved were by turns inflated or deflated. The principal culprit was unquestionably Hugh Fitzjohn Massy, son of John Massy, the latter reputed to be 'a gentleman of good credit and very considerable family in this kingdom'.[1] Some alleged that young Massy had acted entirely of his own volition without any prompting from his family. Whatever misgivings his seniors expressed, they were soon suppressed. The Massys and their connections closed ranks as soon as the Ingoldsbys mobilized their interest to bring the guilty to justice. Rapidly two opposed groupings faced one another. The ability of the Massys and Ingoldsbys respectively to comprehend all of their name and blood in a common stand may be doubted. Over time, nevertheless, a cohesiveness, born of ideology as well as blood, entered into these clans, and governed their responses to the affair of the 1740s. By way of preliminary, therefore, something of the making of the rival dynasties needs to be outlined.

Frances Ingoldsby's forbears had come to Limerick with the Cromwellian siege and capture of the city in 1651. Unlike many other English officers, the two Ingoldsby brothers, Henry and George, stayed on. Henry Ingoldsby had served first as military governor. In 1656, when the charter of the corporation was restored, he was named as mayor. He also represented the area in the Westminster parliaments of the Interregnum. He adjusted easily enough to the restoration of Charles II. In 1661 he was elected to the Dublin House of Commons as knight of the shire for County Clare.[2] Important for the family's permanent attachment to the locality were the marriages of George and Henry Ingoldsby. The latter married a daughter of one of the most important Protestants to have settled in County Limerick before 1641: Sir Hardress Waller.[3] Indeed, during the 1650s Ingoldsby shared the parliamentary representation of the county with his father-in-law. Meanwhile George had also wedded a local heiress, Mary Gould.[4] Thanks to the Cromwellian confiscations and subsequent confirmations after 1660, the Ingoldsbys amassed ample holdings in and around Limerick. Further evidence of the continuing prominence of the two brothers came when George Ingoldsby landed a baronetcy from Charles II and was appointed mayor of the city in 1672.[5]

Eminent though the Ingoldsbys were among the Protestant proprietors of the locality, others overshadowed them. The supple Earl of Orrery, as lord president of Munster until 1672 and governor of the fort of Limerick, interested himself closely in the city, where he had been granted much property. These connections, however, did not survive beyond the life of the first earl.[6] Next, the Southwells, seated at nearby Rathkeale, asserted themselves. Sir Thomas Southwell had precociously and conspicuously championed the Protestant interest in 1688–9. So long as he lived to enjoy the rewards, he constituted a potent link between the locale and the Dublin government, in which he served as a revenue commissioner alongside Speaker Conolly.[7] After he died in 1720, the Southwells, now usually resident at Clontarf in North Dublin, bothered themselves only intermittently with the city. Furthermore, if the Southwells with their estates chiefly situated in the neighbouring county, typified the wish of such landlords to dictate municipal affairs, they were not invariably obeyed.[8] Throughout the early eighteenth century, no single landowner ran the city or controlled its parliamentary seats. Any who aspired to do so had to compete against other landed proprietors and against the complex interests within the city itself. There groups of merchants and professionals had entrenched themselves deeply. The garrison with a strength of more than 1000 had to be reckoned with. In the person of its commander it could exert considerable political influence. Another presence which imbricated Limerick politics was that of the Church of Ireland bishop and cathedral dean and chapter. No lasting equilibrium stilled these competitors. The essential volatility of Limerick politics resembled that of many other

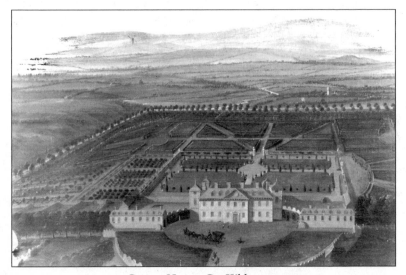

2. Carton House, Co. Kildare, c.1720

sizeable corporations in the early decades of the eighteenth century. The Ingoldsby affair simply re-activated long-standing rivalries.

The Ingoldsbys had reappeared on the public stage in the reign of Queen Anne. Once more two brothers, Sir Richard Ingoldsby and Sir George Ingoldsby, flourished. Warfare – now on the continent, with Marlborough against the French – propelled the Ingoldsbys upwards. Both rose to be generals. Sir Richard Ingoldsby was gazetted lieutenant-general and appointed master of ordnance in Ireland. His high standing was confirmed when he was commissioned as one of the lords justice who headed Ireland's government during the absence of the lord lieutenant. Ingoldsby held this prestigious office from 1709 until he died in 1712. Then he was accorded the rare honour of a state funeral through the streets of Dublin.[9] Commensurate with his new rank and a testimony to the wealth which the family had unobtrusively but steadily accumulated in the intervening years was Sir Richard Ingoldsby's purchase in 1703 of the Talbots' mansion at Carton in County Kildare. He paid £1800 for the house and estate.[10] In addition, the Ingoldsbys owned a Dublin residence, just north of the River Liffey in fashionable Mary Street.[11]

The public standing of the Ingoldsbys depended on Irish and British politics. Their views chimed in with the prevalent Toryism after 1710. Through intricate personal bonds, the Ingoldsbys linked themselves with the like-minded and useful. Their alliances back in the 1650s with the Wallers and Goulds had shown how recent immigrants could embed themselves in the Irish provinces by uniting with the longer established. Further connections acquired early in the eighteenth century explained much of the network which would be activated during the abduction *imbroglio*. First, Barbara, a daughter of Sir George Ingoldsby, married the talented son of a bishop from Ulster. The husband, William Smythe, counted among his numerous cousinage the recently appointed bishop of Limerick, Dr. Thomas Smythe. For his many kinsfolk, William Smythe commanded the qualities of a favourite uncle. In consequence he was entrusted with delicate tasks. Like many another uxorious squire he memorialized his bride, Barbara Ingoldsby, by naming his newly built mansion in Westmeath, Barbavilla. There he oversaw motley business, including from the 1730s the guardianship of his wife's cousin, Frances Ingoldsby.[12] Another of the Ingoldsbys' relations married a rising barrister, Arthur Hasset or Blennerhasset, member of parliament for Tralee.[13] He would share, with William Smythe, care of the Ingoldsby heiresses. Indeed, once Hasset and his wife had settled at Riddlestown, about twelve miles outside Limerick city, the young Frances Ingoldsby would lodge with them.

The third marriage was one through which General Sir Richard Ingoldsby allied his family to that of the most outspoken Tory in the Irish administration of which he himself was a member. From 1710, the Lord Chancellor, Sir Constantine Phipps, a freshly disembarked Englishman, partnered Ingoldsby as lord justice. Phipps' daughter was married to Sir Richard's son and heir,

Henry Ingoldsby. Through the young man the Ingoldsbys' stake in Limerick was put to work for the Tories. In 1713 Henry Ingoldsby was returned to parliament for the corporation: a result earnestly solicited both by his father-in-law, Lord Chancellor Phipps, and by their distant family connection, the Tory bishop of Limerick, Thomas Smythe.[14] Sir Richard Ingoldsby may have projected himself as the unpolitical soldier in the otherwise fiercely partisan Dublin government. In fact, he would hardly have been retained as lord justice had his outlook not pleased the dominant Tories. For Phipps, bent on imposing in Ireland a controversial programme imported from England, the Ingoldsbys furnished excellent channels through which his design could be forwarded. Thanks to the Ingoldsbys the Limerick family of Higgins was brought into Phipps's ambit. In the city, the Ingoldsbys' rents were collected – not always punctually – by an alderman, John Higgins.[15] Higgins's sister, penurious, but with the reputation of being an honest woman, moved to Dublin in order to keep house for General Ingoldsby.[16] A third sibling was the Reverend Francis Higgins, who modelled himself on the darling of the high church party in England, Henry Sacheverell. Like Sacheverell in London, Higgins courted prosecution. Tried for an allegedly seditious sermon he was triumphantly acquitted in 1711.[17]

So long as the Tories ruled in England and Ireland, Irish Protestants of the same kidney, such as the Ingoldsbys, Smythes and Higgins, prospered. But with George I's accession in 1714, such opinions became a liability.[18] Francis Higgins now languished in rural shallows, his passage through the Church of Ireland becalmed.[19] Similarly, Bishop Smythe of Limerick once again found himself the butt of the predominantly Whiggish soldiery of the garrison, and in 1721 was removed from the vice-chancellorship of Dublin University.[20] Alderman Higgins was also a target for Whig animosity in Limerick.[21] Phipps himself returned to England and private practice, lucky not to have been impeached by the Dublin parliament. Soon enough his son-in-law, Henry Ingoldsby no longer an M.P., followed. The latter careered headlong into the pleasures appropriate to 'a young Irish gentleman . . . being in sweet London'.[22] From hired houses in fashionable quarters he indulged in what his Irish rents – calculated in 1713 at £1200 a year – could buy.[23] He had not altogether forgotten Ireland, and not just as the source of his remittances. He shipped back novelties to embellish the house and grounds at Carton.[24] Tongues soon wagged at Ingoldsby's profligacy, so much so that he had to instruct his friends in Ireland, 'I neither keep a whore nor am I parted from my wife'.[25] London delights were taking their toll. Ingoldsby's mind reverted to Ireland, and specifically to Limerick. In 1727 he was once more returned to parliament for the city. He came into the Commons clutching the coat tails of the garrison commander, General Thomas Pearce, who had rapidly but controversially built up his interest within the municipality.[26] If, in the recent past, the garrison had been a bastion of the Whig interest against the Toryism of the established church and a section of the corporation headed by Alderman Higgins, with Pearce these configurations were reversed. The general wrested power from an aggressively Whig oligarchy. To do this he exploited populism and (allegedly) mobilized Catholics. Such tactics, as his adversaries argued, endangered liberty and the 'constitution'. Henry Ingoldsby's own opinions are not recorded. Given his close alliance with and dependence on Pearce, it is probable that in essentials they coincided.[27]

3. Henry Ingoldsby, M.P.

Ingoldsby's revived concern with Limerick owed as much to money as to political ambitions. He was keen to raise his rents there and bring to account the negligent Alderman Higgins.[28] But before he could so, Henry Ingoldsby died, in 1731. He left co-heiresses: his daughters, Catherine and Frances. Although their father's fecklessness had diminished their inheritance, each was regarded as a desirable catch. They were soon besieged by suitors, such as Lord Athenry and the sons of Lord Grandison and Sir Matthew Deane.[29] The less suitable, like Oliver Crofton, also schemed to ensnare the girls. It was even feared than an aspirant might worm his way into the house disguised as a fortune teller.[30] With such perils, the care of the sisters was troublesome. Henry Ingoldsby had named his kinsmen by marriage, William Smythe of Barbavilla and Arthur Hasset, as trustees.[31] Each man through his wife and the terms of Ingoldsby's will had a residual interest in the inheritance should the two girls die without children of their own. In 1734 Catherine was married satisfactorily: to James Lennox Napper, possessor of lands in Meath and Westmeath.[32] Napper may have chosen a bride to shore up his own tottering finances. If this was the calculation, she brought him further liabilities, to escape which (notably Henry Ingoldsby's importunate creditors) Napper removed himself to the continent.[33] What rescued Napper from his difficulties was less his share in the Ingoldsby inheritance than a Gloucestershire estate bequeathed by an uncle on the easy condition that he substitute the patronymic of Dutton for that of Napper.[34] In 1742, his wife died. He was later censured for swiftly remarrying, and to his first wife's companion. Through the son of his first marriage, John Dutton, Napper retained an interest in the fate of the Ingoldsby properties. Indeed, should his sister-in-law, Frances Ingoldsby, fail to bear legitimate issue, then his own son stood to reunite the separated moieties of the Ingoldsby fortune. Intermittently Napper bestirred himself to try to achieve this objective.[35]

The estates inherited by the Ingoldsby sisters in 1731 were heavily encumbered. The Dublin house in Mary Street and its smart furnishings were sold.[36] Carton soon followed: first its contents, and then in 1738 the mansion and lands were bought by the earl of Kildare for £8000.[37] This price represented a good profit on the £1800 paid by Sir Richard Ingoldsby in 1703. Frances, despite the damage wrought by her father's extravagance, was thought in the 1740s still to command about £900 a year. Bees buzzed excitedly around the alluring honey-pot. Efforts were made to diminish the magnetism of the queen bee and her honeycomb by concealing both in an obscure hive. Instead of the high life to which her father had been addicted in London or the hectic sociability of Mary Street and Carton, Frances was buried in the countryside. She boarded with her guardian Hasset and his wife at Riddlestown in County Limerick. Even so she was not entirely denied Dublin society. Hasset, on track for a judgeship on King's Bench, frequented the capital. In 1738, for example, Frances Ingoldsby accompanied the Hassets for a round of plays and

4. Riddlestown House, Co. Limerick

ridottos.[38] She was bound for the same destination in October 1741 when the party stopped first in Limerick city. Hasset halted there in order to participate in the by-election being fought between Alderman Richard Maunsell and Edmund Sexton Pery. Hasset was so much a partisan of Maunsell that he lodged in his house.[39]

Under cover of the excitements of the poll, Frances Ingoldsby had business of her own to transact. Within the household of her father had lived a young man, Jack Williams, a poor relation whom Henry Ingoldsby was prepared to employ and train. Later it was alleged that Ingoldsby had done so because the young man was his bastard son.[40] At all events, Williams was remembered in Ingoldsby's will and kept on as a servant for Frances Ingoldsby.[41] By 1741 the daily intimacies had ripened into a romance. Frances Ingoldsby slipped away from the busy Maunsell house where she was staying with the Hassets. She hurried to an apothecary's house in which Jack Williams's mother lodged. Gathered at the apothecary's were a quack come to cure a growth and his uncle, William Meara, a priest from Borrisokeane. The latter married Jack Williams and Frances Ingoldsby. A modest feast was improvised. A piece of cold beef, bread, saffron cakes, claret and white wine were laid out before a good turf fire. Williams, dissatisfied with the quality of the claret, sent out a servant to buy better. The rites concluded, the girl returned innocently to the Hassets and soon left for Dublin with them.[42] Williams, as a long-serving attendant, stayed within the household. Witnesses would later disagree as to whether or not the marriage had been consummated and whether, albeit in a covert manner, the couple now lived as man and wife.

In retrospect, the accounts concurred that the situation unsettled Frances Ingoldsby's mind, already uneasy. She was said to have rendered herself 'quite stupid' through 'the excess of drinking strong white wines'.[43] She may even have tried to kill herself. In an attempt to recover her health she was sent to lodgings at Dun Laoghaire near Dublin.[44] But she was still in the company of Williams, whose behaviour may either have caused or worsened her distress. Some later reports mentioned his philandering, directed (it was averred) towards fellow servants. Tension also arose because he was worried about the validity of the marriage in Limerick. Frances Ingoldsby had come of age in 1741. Catholic weddings were accepted as legal. However, the circumstances in which it had been performed, with the suspicion of duress, brought into doubt the ceremony. In order to insure against this marriage being annulled, Williams opted for a second. This would be conducted by a Church of Ireland cleric, at an inn, the sign of St. Patrick, near Mount Merrion. However, Frances Ingoldsby jibbed at this proposal. She was upset that the earlier wedding should now be called into question. Her feelings indicated that the marriage had indeed been consummated and that she would now be guilty of fornication. Faced with her refusal, Williams was said to have coerced her.[45]

At this juncture, Frances Ingoldsby's legal custodians, already alarmed by her drinking and instability, intervened. In June 1743, she was snatched from the house in Booterstown where Williams kept her, and taken first to Dublin and next to her brother-in-law's house at Loughcrew. Then, when Napper travelled to England, she was despatched to the rectory at Nantenan. Williams, meanwhile, had been taken before a justice of the peace in the city of Dublin and gaoled at Kilmainham.[46] Following a writ in Chancery he was speedily released. Active in the manoeuvres which sundered the pair were David Bindon, a lawyer with extensive connections in Limerick and Clare;[47] a successful Dublin attorney, William Crookshank, much employed by Napper and the Ingoldsby trustees;[48] and the squire from Baldwinstown, County Dublin, Arthur Mervyn.[49] The last had served as high sheriff for County Dublin during the previous year, and so lent official sanction to the enterprise. When these events were rehearsed in the courts what was at issue was whether or not Frances Ingoldsby had gone voluntarily with Bindon, Crookshank and Mervyn. Some reports emphasized how much force had been used as she was conducted from place to place in a closed coach surrounded with armed men. This forcible seizure could be represented as a kind of abduction. Others, however, thought that Frances Ingoldsby had been glad to be freed from Williams's thrall.[50] Moreover, part of her distress was caused by the liberality with which Williams spread his sexual favours, making no distinction between the servants in the household and his mistress and supposed wife. An erstwhile kitchen maid in the Ingoldsbys' employ, turned off for bearing a child supposedly by the concupiscent Williams, screeched imprecations at Frances

Ingoldsby as she passed through the Dublin streets. 'My curse and the curse of God on you, you bitch of a whore, for putting my poor fellow in gaol'.[51]

In the summer of 1743 those entrusted with the awkward charge of Frances Ingoldsby acted to separate her from Williams. William Smythe and Arthur Hasset wished to free her from any imputation that an unfortunate liaison had been contracted. They planned still to place their valuable prize with the right husband. But hardly had she been parted from Williams and spirited into the countryside when any hope of a suitable match was dashed. She railed against the Limerick seclusion intended to fend off unwanted attentions. Later she would inveigh, 'no farmer's daughter lived in more obscurity than she did'.[52] Being immured with the rector, Royse, and his family at Nantenan was not without its own hazards. Royse's wife was a kinswoman of Frances Ingoldsby. Under the terms of Sir Richard Ingoldsby's will, Mrs Royse had an interest in the disposal of the estate and so, arguably, a wish not to see Frances Ingoldsby produce legitimate children.[53] In addition, Arthur Hasset at nearby Riddlestown was viewed by some as a predator who might himself entrap his well-endowed former lodger. Certainly, when Massy justified his raid on Nantenan, he pictured himself as freeing the vulnerable heiress from the danger of her supposed protectors.[54]

Young Massy knocked up the inmates of the rectory on the dark evening of 13 November 1743. On the pretext of having hurt himself in a fall from his horse he was admitted. Under the threat of violence, he grabbed the booty and made off with it. He was assisted by a brother-in-law, John Bourcher, a 'gentleman' from County Clare, and, like Massy, described as an attorney.[55] Other accomplices included members of the Scanlan and Whelan families.[56] Descriptions of the assault immediately differed as to whether Massy had acted on his own initiative or with the foreknowledge and approval of his relations. It was rumoured that respectable kinsfolk, headed by an uncle, William Massy, disavowed him and were keen to restore Frances Ingoldsby. An alternative version stressed Hugh Fitzjohn Massy's immaturity, and implied that he had been egged on by his elders.[57]

The Reverend Thomas Royse raised the alarm. But with scant resources he felt powerless to contend against the mighty Massy tribe. Royse may have exaggerated his own difficulties to excuse himself to Smythe and Hasset. Yet he and his family before him had been long established in the region and so knew intimately the power of the Massys. A 'desperate band' now bore Frances Ingoldsby into the mountainous country between Limerick and Cork. Royse dared not follow into what he depicted as the stronghold of the Massys and their associates.[58] It is likely that some sort of religious ceremony regularized the position of the couple and induced Frances Ingoldsby to submit to her new husband. Even here, unfortunately, contradictory narratives allow opposed readings. According to some observers, Frances Ingoldsby, assuming her raptor was Jack Williams, expressed her eagerness to quit Nantenan with him. Others, in contrast, even if they allowed that this initial confusion had occurred, insisted that she had willingly succumbed to the sexual prowess of young Massy. Whatever the truth, it was undeniable that Massy had physical control over the young woman.[59] He was proclaimed by the government and a reward of £200 each placed on his and Bourcher's heads. In order to escape, Massy skipped over from Ireland to France. The ease with which he did so, wintering with Frances at Bordeaux, reminded of the easy passages between Cork and the continent and, perhaps, of a community of merchants and exiles into which Massy readily fitted.[60]

Royse, the poor clergyman, bemoaned his impotence in the face of such defiance. He attributed some of the difficulties to the fact that 'most of the first gentlemen' from Counties Limerick and Cork were in Dublin for the start of the parliamentary session.[61] These were the supporters whom Royse might otherwise have used. But, if absent from the locality, these friends of the Ingoldsbys were better placed to enlist the aid of the administration. Miss Ingoldsby's guardians, the influential William Smythe and Arthur Hasset, ensured that the privy council quickly outlawed Massy, Bourcher and their accomplices. There was talk, too, of an act of parliament to bastardize any offspring of the irregular union.[62] However, during the winter of 1743–44, with Massy and his bride in France, little could be done. In any case, rumours of foreign invasion and domestic insurrection gave more pressing priorities to the Irish authorities especially in the maritime counties of the south-west and west like Limerick. One startling gesture expressed the frustration of those anxious to apprehend Massy. Arthur Hasset repudiated any further connection with his wayward ward by selling her clothes at 'public auction'.

Ostensibly this was to cover the money owed for her diet and lodging. It also impressed contemporaries as a sign that the heiress would be disowned by those formerly charged with her welfare.[63] Since the girl had passed so firmly from their control and into Massy's, it was unlikely that she or her fortune could ever be retrieved. Even if Massy was punished and the *mésalliance* sundered, Frances Ingoldsby was now irredeemably tarnished.

The winter while the couple were away in France may have seen some activity by 'Massy's numerous and powerful relations'. Covert preparations in order to secure a sympathetic sheriff who would then empanel an amenable grand jury would make more comprehensible the decision of Hugh Fitzjohn Massy to sail back from France with his bride. With the girl in his power it had been easy enough to persuade her to attest that she had voluntarily married him.[64] Once back in Ireland it was unlikely that he could escape capture. Nor did he seek to do so. Although the outstanding charges had yet to be heard, with a carefully selected jury, Massy might reasonably hope to be acquitted. Certainly this confidence marked his and his wife's public demeanour after their arrival in Limerick. Their bravado affronted the agents

5. Judge Arthur Blennerhasset

of Smythe and Hasset. An augury of what was now to be expected had been offered by the impressive demonstrations which greeted the couple's disembarkation. The bells of St. Mary's cathedral had peeled across the city because an uncle of Massy was its dean. This same uncle, Charles Massy, would busy himself with members of the grand jury in order to urge them to put the most favourable construction on his nephew's impetuosity. Not all within the city took Massy's part. Richard Maunsell, whose election to parliament had been assisted by Hasset in 1741, believed it inappropriate to meet the pair.[65] At first kept in lodgings in Limerick and always surrounded by female Massys,

Frances Ingoldsby (or Massy as perhaps we should now call her) was then removed to the Massys' stronghold in the hills. Remembering the girl's taste for diversions and her impatience with the dullness of Riddlestown and Nantenan, the hopeful predicted that she would rebel against the bucolic regime. But, despite declaring that 'she would not be confined to the company of such dowdies', she never turned against her captor.[66]

From the moment that the news broke that she had been taken to France, her former supporters began to distance themselves. Earlier her wild conduct had been excused but now her character was more systematically besmirched. Shortly after she had arrived from France, it was remarked that 'she behaves with the utmost assurance in all public places'. Back in Limerick, it was regretted that 'her assurance and ignorance was such that I believe she would go to the Castle if she was in Dublin, for she behaves as senseless of her condition as if nothing had befallen her'.[67] So far from displaying a becoming modesty and contrition, she relapsed into habits which had been noticed and criticized in the past. At her Limerick lodgings, 'she sung in company in her uncouth manner as often made modest women blush for it'.[68] Her irritating lack of shame went with a ribald tongue and a fondness for liquor. Such tastes, deemed inappropriate to her gender or station, recalled traits which she had revealed between 1741 and 1743, and perhaps earlier. Detractors raked over her adolescence. She had disparaged the worthy Smythes of Barbavilla when they had sought to restrain her 'from dancing after every fiddle that was played up in the country'.[69] At Barbavilla, too, it was remembered how she had been wont to quaff a pint of wine before dinner, 'thought a bad habit for ladies'.[70] Among the rough Massys these tastes could be fully indulged. In their company at Limerick it was noted that 'she drinks and sings in her cups in her old uncouth manner'.[71] The unfriendliness of these accounts, together with the intention behind them of consciously or unconsciously expelling a disgraced member from the polite company which she had formerly kept, make it impossible to judge their accuracy. Assorted witnesses imputed to her sexual licence, instability and drunkenness. But even if she was guilty of some of these failings, they may have arisen from physical or psychological derangement caused or worsened by the ordeals which she endured.

The composure which Frances Ingoldsby displayed after her return to Limerick was tested by the arrival there of a figure from her past: Jack Williams. Williams insisted on his prior marriage to Miss Ingoldsby. To this end, in August 1744, he began a process in the consistorial court of the bishop of Limerick to prove that they had been married.[72] It failed. Frances Massy never appeared to answer the charge, so that proceedings had regularly to be adjourned, at least until 1750. Williams's meagre means and hopeless position may have reduced him to this strategy. Alternatively, he may have been encouraged by others to initiate the process. The functionaries of the court, from the vicar-general Philip Reidgate, the bishop's commissary John Tunnadine, and the deputy, Arthur Roche, inhabited the same legal, offical and civic worlds as William Smythe, Richard Maunsell and Arthur Hasset.[73] For this reason the court might have been expected to favour Williams. Yet it was powerless to oblige the contumacious Frances Massy to answer. Furthermore, long before 1750, the court's deliberations looked irrelevant to the controversy, the outcome of which had been decided elsewhere.

After his return from the continent, Hugh Massy, together with Bourcher and their principal auxiliaries, were bailed to appear at the assizes. A bill of indictment was heard first at Cork in 1745. Here the activity on Massy's behalf seems to have succeeded. A great concourse pressed round the grand jury-room. Hugh Massy's uncle, Dean Charles Massy, went to work on individual jurors. In consequence the indictment was thrown out.[74] This result seemed to prove what had earlier been asserted about the sinister power exercised by the Massys. Separate charges were then brought at the Limerick assizes for Trinity 1745. At first it looked as if the rigour applied by the judge sent from Dublin would defeat the Massys' local following. One of the two judges appointed to the circuit was Arthur Hasset. In view of his deep involvement, he left the Massy case to his colleague, William Yorke. Yorke may have had vestigial ties with the city of Limerick, but these had weakened.[75] He had arrived in Ireland eager to apply his ideals of impartiality, and these he brought with him to Limerick. Faced with Massy and Bourcher, Judge Yorke demanded to know why they had been bailed and were now placed at a side bar in the court-room rather than in the dock 'among the rest of the felons'. The judge then thundered at Bourcher as he nonchalantly cracked nuts throughout the proceedings. Yorke promptly fined the sheriff £200 for his misconduct of the case and ordered that the two be held in custody until the next assize.[76] However, when that hearing started, no one pressed the charge.[77] Massy and Bourcher were accordingly freed, and the legality of the former's marriage to Frances Ingoldsby was accepted.

It may be that the man on whom the burden of prosecuting the suit fell, the Reverend Thomas Royse, tired of the cause. Royse lacked money; he may also have been failing in health since in 1747 he died.[78] He had been pressed, whether simply on his own account or for those whom he represented (notably Smythe and Hasset) to compound with the Massys. Other evidence also hinted that the Massys were prepared to buy off adversaries rather than face the tedious uncertainties of the legal system. Thus the upright William Smythe of Barbavilla had been approached by one of Massy's counsel, Francis Geoghegan, with an offer of two-thirds of Frances Ingoldsby's property if the charges were abandoned. At this juncture, Smythe refused to be suborned.[79] But Royse may have been more yielding, especially as the likelihood of defeating the Massys receded.

The Massys, having gained physical control over the heiress, took over her estate. Under the terms of her father's will of 1731, the girl was to receive

£3000 on marriage as well as half his property.[80] Whether by the 1740s suf-
ficient money remained to pay the portion is uncertain. What is clear is the
access which Hugh Ingoldsby now acquired to the Limerick estates of his
wife. Yielding above £870 annually, they materially altered his condition.
From being a cadet of a collateral branch of the senior Massy line obliged to
follow the precarious calling of an attorney, he now set up on his own as a
landowner. Something of his change in circumstances was shown when he
dropped the ubiquitous style of 'gentleman' in favour of that of 'esquire'.[81]
Some of the Ingoldsby fortune was quickly invested in improvements to his
holdings near Ballylanders in the southern uplands of County Limerick, close
to the Glen of Aherlow. In 1750 he was granted the right to hold a fair near
Massy Lodge, on a site named Anglesborough.[82] This sounds like a phonetic
acknowledgment of the source of his new riches: Anglesborough, a rendering
of Ingoldsby. But although he now passed as a squire in county society, mem-
ories of the escapade lingered. Critics repeatedly decried the brazen fashion
in which Frances Massy had comported herself. In 1746 she was confronted
unexpectedly by Judge Hasset and his family as they were entering the church
at Rathkeale. Frances Massy was so startled that she had to be supported by

6. Massy Lodge,
Anglesborough,
Co. Limerick

7. Memorial to Hugh Ingoldsby Massy, 1771

her brother-in-law. It was gleefully reported that 'she appeared in some confusion and she looks much paler and thinner than ever she did'.[83] Frances Massy died in 1755.[84] How much the sequence of events had scarred her, mentally, bodily or in reputation, can only be guessed. She had first borne Massy a daughter and then a son, Hugh Ingoldsby Massy.[85] As late as 1777 it was contended that the latter's illegitimacy was 'a matter of great notoriety in Limerick'.[86] Be that as it may it did not prevent the son from inheriting in 1770, nor from serving as high sheriff the next year.[87] His death in 1771 delivered the estate to a baby, fruit of the union between Hugh Ingoldsby Massy and Ann Nash. The father of the latter, James Nash, as grand-father and guardian of the infant owner, jealously defended the property against those with claims on it through descent from William Smythe, James Lennox Dutton or Mrs Anabella Royse. The allegations of Jack Williams, more than thirty years old, were resuscitated. In the interval positions had been reversed. The now respected Massys represented the incumbents who were preyed upon by the aggressive and powerful Nash.[88]

In the minds of opponents such as the Smythes and Hassets, Hugh Fitzjohn Massy and his successors dwelt on the edges of social acceptability. But no matter how much the party of Smythe, Hasset and Ingoldsby might deride the Massys, the last were neither survivors from an archaic order nor rude upstarts. The Massys' line in Ireland was coeval with that of the Ingoldsbys.[89] Yet associated with the hilly country on the borders of Limerick and Cork, fastnesses into which their lowland competitors dared not venture, they were portrayed as 'a wicked, numerous and powerful faction', almost as savages.[90] In actuality, while Hugh Massy had carried his prize into the uplands and later kept her there during his trial, the Massys had long been colonizing the fertile basin of the Shannon where the Smythes, Ingoldsbys, Royses and Hassets were seated. The notion of ecological determinism, with the remote habitations of the Massys explaining their cultural primitivism, has some plausibility for Hugh Fitzjohn Massy but little for the generality of his family such as the future Baron Duntrileague or his accomplished uncle, Dean Charles Massy. Already in the 1740s the dynasty possessed great weight, as their manoeuvres over the abduction case demonstrated. Thereafter they steadily enhanced their standing. Massys were frequently included in the commission of the peace; several served as high sheriffs. In 1759 one was elected to parliament for the county; in 1776 the family was ennobled as Barons Duntrileague.[91]

The Massys' integration into the local ruling elite sat awkwardly with the armed raid on Nantenan, and the subsequent efforts to avoid punishment for it. The Massys, like others entrusted with authority in the localities, were adept at the controlled use of force. In 1722 the senior Massy of Duntrileague commanded the militia and distinguished himself by harrying Catholics.[92] The trouble was the shifting line between authorized and unsanctioned violence. Recourse to force, even by the mid-eighteenth century, was not reserved to the excluded or dispossessed. The tory or highwayman shaded imperceptibly into the buccaneers who pursued the enemies of the Protestant state or of their affinities. The band which had ambushed Frances Ingoldsby could be depicted as dangerous, but it differed little from others which elsewhere seized heiresses. More pertinently, perhaps, the methods employed at Nantenan were not so different from those used to rescue Frances Ingoldsby from Jack Williams in Dublin during the summer of 1743. Both might be seen as armed raids.[93]

The menace with which the hostile invested the contingent which had grabbed Frances Ingoldsby derived not just from the numbers and weapons. Several of the assistants bore names – Michael Scanlan, Tim Crimmin [Cremin?], James Curran and Bonaventure Kenny – which implied Irish and Catholic ancestry.[94] Later it would be rumoured that Massy himself died a Catholic. Such innuendoes, intended to add to the mistrust of the Massys and relax their hold over the Ingoldsby estate, caused little harm. John Bourcher, for example, insisted that he had been raised as a Protestant.[95] He suffered no derogation for his part in the abduction, although said to be guilty of another three rapes. Bourcher was favoured by his brother-in-law, Massy, with a rent charge of £100 a year on Ingoldsby properties, perhaps to recompense him for his aid. Thus assisted, Bourcher, like Massy, moved from the ranks of the gentry into the squirearchy.[96] Similarly Michael Scanlan not only conformed to the state church, but hoped for admission into the innermost county elite.

In 1759 when he sought a Southwell to second his request to be made a justice of the peace, he acknowledged that his request might be hampered by 'my wildness in former days . . . fearing I may make bad use of it'.[97] Ambivalence towards the law among those entrusted with its enforcement and operations lay at the heart of Protestant Ireland, as the seemingly routine involvement of so many of the propertied in episodes like the Ingoldsby rape showed. The consciously respectable, led by Smythe, Hasset and Royse, might endeavour to differentiate themselves and their attitudes from those of the Massys through a greater willingness to obey the laws. In practice, the differences were hardly absolute. The likes of Smythe and Hasset, well placed as legislators and legists, bent the system to their needs. Yet for all their acuity, they were unable to defeat the Massys, either on the ground or in the courts of Limerick.

In the charges and counter-charges traded during the affair, little was made of confessional or ethnic differences between the adversaries. It could be that the accusations of primitivism against the Massys implied values associated with the Catholic Irish. However, as we have seen, the Massys' backgrounds lent little credence to such assumptions. Furthermore, the enemies of the Massys may have been reticent about using such tactics for fear that much might then be made of the strong Catholic links of Jack Williams. The group which Williams assembled to witness his wedding in Limerick in 1741 included several of his kindred, among them the officiating priest.[98] Later, while pursuing his case in the bishop's court he sheltered with his Fitzgerald relations at Glin. Also, he entrusted vital documents to the custody of the Knight of Glin.[99] Much of his world was Catholic. His first marriage had been a Catholic ceremony. Whatever oscillations followed, he returned to catholicism when he wrote his will in 1782. He asked then that three masses be said over his body and that his name be entered in the mass-book so that he could be prayed for. He requested that his corpse be kept for forty-eight hours before being buried at Killpatrick near Castle Pollard, presumably so that he could be waked.[100]

Provincial Lives

One benefit of the spasmodically full documentation of the Ingoldsby affair is the beam which it shines into otherwise obscure lives. Jack Williams, partly because he survived longest among the principals – probably until 1782 – was most obviously damaged. The Massys advertised his death in the Limerick newspapers in 1744.[1] This ploy was intended to persuade Frances Ingoldsby to abandon all hope of returning to his bed. Exiguous resources forced him to drop his suit in the Limerick consistory court. Instead he was imprisoned in the Dublin Marshalsea for fifteen years.[2] There he relied on the charity of some, notably the attorney William Crookshank and William Smythe, who in 1743 had prised him away from Frances Ingoldsby.[3] Later those with a continuing claim to the Ingoldsby inheritance – William Smythe and his son, Ralph Smythe, through the former Barbara Ingoldsby; John Dutton through his mother Catherine Ingoldsby; Thomas Henry Royse through his mother; even Thomas Ingoldsby in Buckinghamshire – used Williams. If the fact and validity of his marriage, either in 1741 or 1743, could be proved, now that Frances Massy was dead and without any children by Williams, then these residuary legatees might negate the Massys' title to the Ingoldsby estate. Williams, broken by long imprisonment and an alcoholic, tried to profit from this situation. Once released from gaol he had shifted as best he could to live. Initially he had been engaged by another inmate of the Marshalsea, Arthur Rochfort, brother of the infamous Lord Belfield, to tutor some of his children.[4] This unlikely job had not lasted long. Instead Williams could make money either by proving his marriage or keeping quiet about it. In particular, once James Nash in the name of his grandson, Hugh Ingoldsby Massy, asserted the Massy claim, Williams felt himself to be at risk from 'diverse persons of great power and influence in the said county and city of Limerick'. He protected himself by depositing the papers most germane to the marriage with the Knight of Glin.[5]

Nash stifled Williams's inconvenient claim to have been married first to Frances Ingoldsby by lodging him with an innkeeper at Millstreet in the north of County Cork. Through the innkeeper, William Cotter, Nash allowed Williams a weekly 5s 9d. By controlled doles of drink and money, Nash hoped to edge Williams into signing a declaration that he had in fact married one of the Ingoldsbys' servants, Margaret Branagan, not the mistress.[6] Nash went to these lengths so long as John Dutton threatened to use Williams for the opposite purpose: namely, to invalidate the Massy marriage and so disinherit Hugh Ingoldsby Massy. At one point Dutton apparently brought Williams over to England. However, Dutton's death ended this particular threat. It was immediately replaced by a similar claim advanced by Ralph Smythe and Thomas Henry Royse. Williams exploited his pivotal position. Latterly supplied with housing, tobacco, newspapers and drink by the Smythes of Barbavilla he cut a sorry figure.[7] In 1777 he himself confessed how he had been driven into 'those cursed drunken passions which destroyed my soul, body, life and health'.[8]

Williams gravitated to the *menu peuple* and servants. Without any adequate patrimony, his predicament could be said to resemble that of Hugh Fitzjohn Massy. Dr. Anthony Malcomson in his far-reaching investigations of the quest for heiresses concluded that the like circumstanced were coupled with like.[9] But both Williams and Massy believed that an advantageous match could mend their finances. For Massy it certainly did; the ruined Williams dragged his disappointments with him to the grave. In youth, brighter prospects had beckoned. Kinship with the Ingoldsbys had led to his being plucked from provincial indigence. Through his mother Williams was descended, like Henry Ingoldsby himself, from Sir Thomas Browne of Hospital in County Limerick.[10] On its own this lustrous pedigree left Williams only with pretensions which he could not sustain. It did, however, ally him with numerous others in the region, who assisted his scheme to marry Frances Ingoldsby. Some of this kindred assembled in the apothecary's premises for Williams's wedding in October 1741. They included female cousins bred as maids in the households of wealthier relations, who kept shops or patched together a pittance with their needles. William Meara, the priest who conducted the ceremony, was also related to Williams.[11]

Williams himself, and his contemporaries, stressed his humble condition. This fact readily explained why he had been outwitted by the Massys with their superior resources. Such an explanation is not altogether convincing. Covertly at first, and then openly, Williams's allegations were backed by others with heavier purses: the Smythes, Duttons and James Nash. Nor, indeed, can an absolute contrast be drawn between the modesty of Williams's connections and means and the amplitude of Hugh Fitzjohn Massy's. The latter's expectations as the son of a cadet of the increasingly prolific Massy clan cannot now be ascertained. However, his choice of the calling of an attorney indicated a need to supplement whatever revenues he drew from inherited property. Moreover, other cadets of like condition formed the gang which nabbed Frances Ingoldsby. But Massy's supporters were not limited to the landed of Limerick. Also implicated were a William Massy, 'merchant' of Dublin, together with a tailor and shoemaker from the capital. Massy, although rooted in the countryside, was no stranger to the town.[12]

Throughout his early years Williams's habitat had been the Ingoldsby household. The intimacies of daily life stimulated this Lothario. Pregnancies and jealousies resulted. Privacy was well-nigh impossible to achieve in the cramped and ramshackle houses of the time, even of the grand. So, when his conduct was scrutinized in the courts, the aggrieved attested to his failings. A domestic from the Hassets' seat at Riddlestown announced that she had espied Frances Ingoldsby and Jack Williams through a key-hole. The girl might have caught only a hazy impression of the couple in bed together. Nevertheless, she identified Williams conclusively thanks to his hastily cast-off clothes. In particular, she recognized the shoe-buckles, 'which were remarkable'.[13] Vanity in this article seems to have affected other men of humble station eager to impress would-be partners, and reminds how servants in apeing the modes of their employers speeded the transmission of fashions.[14] A housemaid had surprised the pair naked in bed, 'very loving together'.[15] A third servant had similarly caught them *in delicto flagrante*. She was given a guinea by Frances Ingoldsby to keep her peace.[16] The sense of watchers well able to remember what they had seen, especially when memory was jogged by payments, recurred. In 1766, a tailor's wife, Sarah Madden, recalled how, 'the year after the Great Frost', in 1741, she had observed the marriage ceremony in Limerick 'through a chink in the wainscoat'. Other servants and tradespeople were pressed, as late as the 1770s, to cast back their minds to what they had witnessed, either at the apothecary's or in Dublin in 1743.[17]

Much of the testimony came from women. Both as victims of Williams's satyriasis and as voyeurs in the various houses they were well situated to tell what had happened. In general, the accounts reveal women as passive receptors of the physical and legal tyranny of men. As sustained efforts were made to blacken the character of the lost Frances Ingoldsby, it was hinted that through her libidinous behaviour she had provoked her tormentors. It could be that she, like her mother before her, violated the codes of the day and sought to choose for herself her sexual partners.[18] But women were also complicit in the conspiracies of Williams and Massy. In 1741, after all, it was Williams's mother, Annabella Forster, who supplied the *venue* in Limerick where the precipitate marriage was solemnized. Other women were willingly present. Later, in 1743, when Frances Ingoldsby was hustled away from Williams, she was incarcerated first in lodgings kept by a Mrs Pollard in Abbey Street in Dublin, yet another of the kinsfolk of the Ingoldsbys who could be mobilized.[19] Even Mrs Royse, the rector's wife at Nantenan, assumes a more sinister guise. Not only did she have a claim on the Ingoldsby lands through her mother, but neighbours regarded her as malevolently meddlesome when it came to match-making.[20] Nor was Arthur Hasset's wife necessarily a passive spectator in all that occurred under her roof. Frances Ingoldsby herself had declared that Mary Hasset was 'both master and mistress' in the household.[21] Then, in 1745, female Massys were the 'dowdies' who pinioned the young heiress lest she fly to Williams or her own relations.[22] The powerlessness of wronged women to defeat their abductors, whether through physical retaliation or legal proceedings, is strongly conveyed by the Ingoldsby affair. Other than to slip out to the apothecary's in October 1741, Frances Ingoldsby seldom moved freely. Moreover, once she became disputed property this little liberty was curtailed. Such inhibitions were common. It can be replicated from the example of a recently married woman in County Wexford. Nelly Ball, quickly separated from her husband, pleaded in the 1750s to be allowed her annuity by her in-laws so that she could join her husband overseas.[23] More striking still is the example of Frances Bellew in 1729. Her misfortunes began when a brother-in-law gained control over the annual allowance of £150 to which she was entitled under her mother's will. Could she but recover this income, she planned 'to live like a private gentlewoman', perhaps in Dublin or preferably at Chester. Above all she needed to escape from her brother-in-law. For four years he had kept her in Connacht among his own people, 'incognito, unknown to my relations'. So long as she was denied her annuity she could do nothing. Her chance came when she was brought to Dublin. There she managed to take lodgings on her own account and regularly stood 'at the windows to show all my friends where I am, in hopes some would come to see justice done me'. Yet still she could only display herself, not go to her own kinsfolk.[24]

Frances Bellew's appearances at the windows of her Dublin rooms uncannily prefigured those of Frances Ingoldsby when in Limerick. Glimpses of the latter were breathlessly reported to the interested; so too the attendant bevy of female Massys.[25] These examples merely confirm the tendency of the time to treat propertied women primarily as chattels. It could be that the independent-minded Frances Ingoldsby had chafed against such treatment. In marrying the insinuating Jack Williams she may have acted in obedience to her own wishes. Such assertiveness, if such it was, so far from being commended, was quickly incorporated into a personification which dwelt on the unbecoming and subversive. Frances Ingoldsby's erstwhile protectors transformed her into a figure dominated by sexual appetite, drunkenness and the manic. In this guise she was the more easily degraded from the company of the respectable and abandoned to the supposedly barbaric Massys. How she then fared in the bucolic setting of Anglesborough we do not know. Among her blood relations and youthful companions, the image of the vivacious virgin was replaced by that of the unbalanced hoyden.

The characterization of Frances Ingoldsby paralleled that of Hugh Massy and Jack Williams. Each is known only from unfriendly testimony generally constructed by lawyers for legal purposes. Through their contrived questions and answers evidence was elicited which confirmed the presuppositions about the three main actors in the story. With Williams, his low condition readily explained his boldness in inveigling his mistress into a clandestine liaison. To the picture of the unscrupulous adventurer were added plausible details of sexual promiscuity. Once he took to drink, it was scarcely necessary to remind that he was too erratic to be trusted. Frances Ingoldsby was rapidly made into the embodiment of flightiness, who might well have provoked what she received. The third character, Hugh Fitzjohn Massy, remained the least substantial. This may reflect the intention of his enemies, happy to denote him as a marionette jerked by his seniors. Only in the aftermath of the case does he materialize into a figure dangerous in his own right. At the Mallow races in 1746 he was said to have struck and killed a jockey of Matthews of Thomastown with his weighted whip. Immediately Massy was seized by two Newcomens. They shouted that, if he had been saved from the gallows once, now he ought to swing.[26] The fracas subsided; the jockey was not dead. But the ugly scene reminded of the continuing antagonisms between the gentry of the locality, which the Ingoldsby entanglement had served only to aggravate.[27]

Hugh Massy tended to be subsumed into the rest of his dynasty. The Massys were repeatedly portrayed as dangerous. The Ingoldsbys' allies on the spot had immediately excused their own feeble response to the raid at Nantenan because the 'Massys are so numerous and so rich and have so much land every where in those parts that every one is intimidated'.[28] Such forebodings persisted. When, in 1777, endeavours were renewed to wrest his property from Hugh Ingoldsby Massy, it was acknowledged that his relationship with the 'numerous and powerful family of Massys in the said county' would be hard to overcome, 'and that most of the freeholders in the said county are their tenants, relations or friends'.[29] With their extended kindred, the Massys resembled the Gaelic septs. Also, in way of life and values they recalled those whom they had supplanted. Often it was stressed how the desperadoes had vanished into the mountains with Frances Ingoldsby, in their eyrie secure from pursuers. Into the same fastnesses the dispossessed Irish gentry had retreated. In addition, these havens sheltered tories, raparees, highwaymen and the others who rattled the Hanoverian state in Ireland. As we have seen, notwithstanding a bid to fix on the Massys attributes inimical to the civility, order and industry beloved of the authorities, many of the Massys were pillars of the Protestant interest in the plain around Limerick city.

What dismayed their opponents particularly was the ease with which the Massys manipulated the local legal machine. Mindful of their malign influence, vain efforts were made to have the indictments against Massy and his con-federates heard outside the region, preferably in Dublin. Judge Hasset had exploited his considerable influence to this end, but fruitlessly. As late as 1777, it was felt that only before a 'jury of some indifferent county' would there be any likelihood of defeating the Massys' combination.[30] These fears were understandable: the juries in Cork and Limerick dismissed the charges. The Massys benefited from the favour of the county governor, Lord Southwell, and the sheriff, John Evans, his agents, and the grand jurors themselves. Furthermore, the throng which assembled outside the court-houses during the assizes while Massy's fate was decided recalled older practices. In 1608, the Dublin administration had been warned about troubles in Connacht, 'when the lords and gentlemen meet upon the parley hills, he is accounted the bravest man that comes attended with most of those followers'.[31] The authorities in Dublin looked askance at aristocrats who maintained and were attended by elaborate retinues. At the same time, however, the state valued the numerous tenants and followers which the well-established could command, especially at moments of emergency when the island needed to be defended. Because of the continuing unsettledness of Ireland throughout the eighteenth century, the military functions of lordship persisted. So long as local notables did not defy the government overtly, the use of tenants and dependents to further personal vendettas was connived at. Between the 1690s and the mid-eighteenth century, contemporaries attested to the menacing contingents which could be deployed in their localities by magnates such as the Wynnes in Sligo, Rochforts and Handcocks in Westmeath or the Massys in Limerick.[32] In this what is striking is not just the persistence of habits which elsewhere because both archaic and dangerous had been outlawed, but the ability of recently established families to construct such interests. They, like their predecessors, organized their power through their own ramifying lines and those others linked by marriage, tenancies or simple calculus. Administrators and some judges worried about the capacity of the locally mighty to vary the uniform operations of the distant state for their own advantage. Certainly cases of partisan sheriffs, partial magistrates and subservient jurors abounded throughout the eighteenth century.[33]

The demonization of the Massys told more of the frustrations of their opponents than of the objective facts of the Massys' condition. The headstrong Hugh Massy might personify the lusts of youth and the desperation of the half-mounted without enough land to buy the life of a gentleman for himself. But, whatever detractors might say, he did not epitomize the manners of all Massys. No less than the allied Ingoldsbys, Smythes, Hassets and Royses, the Massys were infiltrating the apparatus of the Protestant state in Ireland. In doing so they readily took on some of the necessary colouration of urbanity, politeness and civility. One uncle of the impetuous young blood, William Massy, acted vigorously against alleged abductors.[34] At the same time, however, members of the family retained their own distinctive attributes. The cultural ambiguities in these reciprocal processes are illustrated by another of their name, Charles Massy. As uncle of the malefactor and dean of Limerick, Charles Massy busied himself on behalf of his errant nephew. In this crisis, family feeling overpowered any loyalty to more abstract concepts. Thus the dean went to work to persuade grand jurors of his nephew's innocence. He may also have pressed his clerical subordinate, Thomas Royse, not to persist with the charges. Dean Massy, nevertheless, united this passionate family attachment with other sentiments. In 1731 a by-election to replace Henry Ingoldsby as member for the city divided the neighbourhood. Charles Massy

voted for Charles Smythe, a son of the former bishop.[35] In doing so he backed
the Church interest. Unwittingly perhaps he aligned himself with the
remnants of the old Tory alliance which now coalesced around Smythe. By
the time of the 1761 election, the candidate who stood against Smythe was
the dean's own son, Hugh Dillon Massy. Understandably the father now voted
for his own.[36] In truth Dean Massy straddled several worlds, and without any
obvious sense of discomfort: of professionals, the educated, traders and
craftsmen in the city and the rural squirearchy. In his deanery he dispensed
abundant hospitality, as one appreciative English visitor remarked during the
1750s, and thereby met the obligations which the absent bishop so notoriously
neglected.[37] Within the city, the only rival centre of elegant entertainment was
the Smythes' house. There the itinerating lord lieutenant was feted and feasted
in 1755.[38] Charles Massy belonged to the city and espoused its values. But he
also knew and understood the county gentry, many of whose priorities and
customs he shared. His main residence was at Doonass in County Clare. Here
he patronized the legendary harper, Carolan.[39] Concurrently, through his
office, he led the regular worship of the Protestant cathedral in Limerick. In
the corporation he emerged as the scourge of corruption. He attacked in print
the civic oligarchy, composed largely of allies of the Ingoldsbys and Smythes.
On the strength of his shrewdly publicized campaign, the dean has been
praised recently as a provincial Charles Lucas and a 'Whiggish idealist'.[40]

The Whiggery of the dean, as of the rest of his tribe, can hardly be gainsaid.
However, it went with an attitude towards some aspects of the Protestant state
in Ireland so cavalier as to weaken and baffle it. This was the more ironical as
Massy denounced the self-interest of Limerick's rulers. In doing so he
appealed to the larger community of the freemen assembled in the court of
d'oyer hundred (deer hundred), as earlier the Tory-inclined General Pearce
and Henry Ingoldsby had. Massy's villains in the 1740s – David Bindon the
lawyer; Alderman Richard Maunsell, member of parliament, and Jacques
Ingram, the diocesan schoolmaster – prided themselves on their modern
manners. As agents of Smythe and Hasset they had also led the attack on
Hugh Fitzjohn Massy. Dean Massy, in the hope of ousting the clique, engaged
his friends among the country gentry. According to Massy's propaganda the
town, in Ireland for so long treasured as a bastion of order and virtue in an
unruly island, was now condemned as the seat of contagion. True freedom, he
contended, would be restored only when the independent and uncorrupted
landowners intervened in the running of the city.[41] Specifically he turned to
the Southwells, the Burtons of Buncraggy in County Clare and the O'Briens
of Dromoland to redress the balance and revive civic integrity. Some at least
of the same group had been mobilized on behalf of the dean's wayward
nephew. The sympathy of Lord Southwell had been important in thwarting
Smythe's and Hasset's attack on Hugh Fitzjohn Massy. The amity between the

Southwells and Massys was further suggested when in 1759, after the sitting Southwell had died, Hugh Massy of Duntrileague was elected to parliament in his stead.[42]

The Massys, never having dallied with Toryism, were reputed staunch Whigs, as were the Southwells. The Ingoldsbys, in contrast, at the beginning of the century were in the thick of Tory politics. Much of their residual connection in and around Limerick consisted of the fragments from that once powerful political and familial affinity, concentrated especially in the church and municipality. It retained good connections in the higher reaches of the Dublin administration. Even within Limerick, although the Ingoldsby interest enfolded the Smythes, Bindons, Maunsell and Ingram, it did not monopolize the allegiance of the local oligarchs. Dean Massy himself showed how prominent clergymen could adhere to an alternative group. Nevertheless, and perhaps for no better reasons than that the bulk of the Ingoldsby estate was in or near the city, it was there that their support was strongest. This situation implied a weaker hold over the country gentry. Certainly, on the evidence of the Ingoldsby affair, the Massys were better able to enlist help from the county. Such divergences accentuated the tendency of the upholders of the Ingoldsby cause, because they dwelt mainly in the town, to represent themselves as embarked on a campaign in which urban virtues, of a civil and anglicized order, warred against the anarchy – and by extension the Irishness – of the rural population. This was an arresting banner under which to march. Its effectiveness was, however, somewhat lessened by the activities of Dean Massy, so prominent in the opposing ranks. He proclaimed similar beliefs, but called on an independent gentry to rout venal townsmen.

In tactics little distinguished the two sides. Other than in kidnapping Frances Ingoldsby, the Massys seldom flouted the law. Thanks to their local strength, they did not need to do so. They may have lacked the elevated links with the Dublin government of William Smythe, a respected member of parliament, or of Arthur Hasset, newly installed as a judge in King's Bench. The Massys as a result could not quickly turn for help to parliament, council or courts. Where they prevailed was in the control of the local agencies through which the decrees of central government were executed. By these means, Hugh Fitzjohn Massy was acquitted first in Cork and then in Limerick, and gained Frances Ingoldsby. Such triumphs should warn against contemplating only what was being done in Dublin, and so mistaking the theory for the practice of power in provincial Ireland.

Local and National Politics

By setting the abduction in social and political contexts, it has been implied that it was not an aberration from the routines of provincial life. Furthermore, it has been suggested, the incident continued a competition of considerable antiquity. The causes of the antipathies, and the reasons why the Ingoldsby incident aggravated them, need now to be addressed.

The most persuasive analyses of Irish parliamentary politics before 1760 have differentiated a phase of extreme polarization in the reign of Queen Anne from the confusions which preceded and succeeded. In essentials, the politics of Limerick conformed to this pattern. Differences in outlook and affiliation among the Protestants of the area owed much to tradition, inherited and newer rivalries and the spur of self-interest. Often they reflected the varied responses to the successive crises which had engulfed locals in virtually every decade between the 1640s and 1690s. By the last years of the seventeenth century, activists tended to align themselves either with the 'court' or the 'country'. After 1702, however, these loose agglomerations hardened into the rigid groupings of 'Whig' and 'Tory'.[1] In Limerick, the axis of Higgins, Ingoldsby, Smythe and Phipps thrived under the Tory pennant. Ideology and interest, as well as temperament and history, separated this group from its Whig opponents. The discrete elements which composed Protestant Limerick might have been expected to adopt particular political stances. Since the Tories prided themselves on their devotion to the privileges of the established Church, the clergy might reasonably side with them. Apparently opposed to them, as passionate defenders of the Revolution, its settlement seemingly jeopardized by the uncertainties over a Protestant succession after 1710, were the officers of the garrison. In practice, none of the institutions of the city, be it corporation, garrison or Church of Ireland clergy, unanimously backed a single party.

Not only was Protestant opinion fragmented, it was mutable. A determined individual, notably the military governor, Pearce, in the 1720s or later Dean Charles Massy, swung the garrison or the cathedral chapter away from its old and into a new political orientation. Thus, while tradition mattered in the formation of political allegiances, the latter were not fixed, and could be modified when fresh issues came into debate or impressive new leaders arose. Nor were kinship, heredity, neighbourhood or the memory of old obligations always proof against the erratic effects of temperament and belief. For the minority regularly involved in politics, choices had constantly to be made.

These were not confined to the irregular parliamentary elections, but could focus on filling vacancies in the corporation, the selection of the high sheriff and the nomination of grand and petty jurors. Indeed, as the official agencies of the Hanoverian state proliferated, service as a commissioner on turnpike trusts, seats on the Linen' Barrack and Inland Navigation boards or an office in the revenue were all eagerly sought.[2] Who was appointed mattered. For the successful a prospect of prosperity beckoned. The disappointed might feel slighted and aggrieved. The outcome also affected the patrons. Materially, by placing more of their clients, the opportunities for profit were enhanced: a road in consequence could be routed advantageously; a barrack conveniently located; or a better supply of flax seed, spinning wheels and looms procured. Decisions were also read as all too public registers of the relative standing of local rivals.

Many preferred not to have to choose between alternatives, knowing the likelihood of giving offence or rupturing friendships. In this spirit, the frequency and ferocity of elections were reprobated. Here the unpolitical or idealistic mistook elections as the cause rather than merely a result of the local antagonisms. The philosophy and stance of independence attracted these non-combatants. But the vaunted independence, while at best it allowed freedom to decide each question on its merits, concealed a multiplicity of often partisan attitudes. It offered, for example, an acceptable cover for those once Tory, who, no longer able to proclaim such dangerous allegiances, nevertheless wanted to re-enter public life. In Limerick the vitality of the once rampant Tory interest showed in the heated election of 1727, when Pearce and Ingoldsby were elected. Subtly transmuted, it underpinned Charles Smythe, occupant of one of the city seats in parliament from 1731, and assisted others who allied with Smythe, notably Edmund Sexten Pery.[3] It also supplied the kernel of the ruling clique in the municipality, against which Dean Massy railed in the 1740s and 1750s. The problem in the transformation, both at the national level and in Limerick, was to discern what had become of the ideological cohesiveness which had previously united the Tories and made them so formidable. Little now separated the different and shifting groupings in parliament, since almost all upheld the legal privileges of the established Church, defended the inviolability of the Revolution settlements and scrutinized the activities of the administration with critical loyalty.

The confusing situation in Limerick by the 1730s and 1740s, the skeletal remains of older configurations occasionally visible behind more recent concerns, supports the characterizations of parliamentary politics after 1714 by Dr. David Hayton.[4] The reasonably tight discipline of Whig and Tory mutated into a more fluid politics. The participants chased power, place and profit. Power was sought in order to worst adversaries, to impress actual and potential followers – in the localities as much as in parliament itself – and for what might then be done with it. This quest among the able and ambitious for pre-eminence did not automatically drive out principle. Issues persisted, such as how Catholic and Protestant dissenters were to be treated or how to deal with the executives in Dublin and London, on which responses differed. Yet these were no longer such pervasive worries as to determine stance for much more than a single parliamentary session. Except at the moments of high excitement, such as the crises over Wood's Halfpence in 1723–5 and the Money Bill in 1753, members were free to run after those to whom they were attached already by blood, tradition, geography or education.[5] Thus, in the decades after 1714 locality, heredity and kinship were the spindles around which the main political groupings turned. In many features, the squadrons now commanded by the most effective commanders, such as the Boyles, Brodricks, Conolly, Gores and Ponsonbys, were successors to the apanages and affinities of the earlier Anglo-Irish magnates like Kildare, Ormond and Desmond. A marked change by the early eighteenth century was the greater weight exerted by Ulster. An influx from the north-west in particular, led by William Conolly but including an interrelated clan of Leslies, Conynghams, Cairnes, Hamiltons, Gores and Nesbitts, first colonized lucrative branches of the Dublin administration, established members in the business and banking worlds of London, bought up confiscated estates in the Pale to the north of Dublin and by the 1720s dominated the Irish parliament.[6] Because so triumphant, measures which were carried during the ascendancy of this connection, like the statutes which directed taxes towards the linen industry or the construction of roads, canals and bridges, were criticized by the members from the three other provinces as favouring Ulster. These political groupings, essentially personal and dependent on outstanding leaders, proved kaleidoscopic and unstable. The prolonged succession disputes when Speaker Conolly died or Speaker Boyle was undermined recalled those which had so frequently convulsed the earlier Anglo-Norman and Gaelic lordships. These instabilities added to the uncertainties of eighteenth-century politics and the troubles of the successive lords lieutenant who had to handle them.

Limerick lacked a single dominant political ruler. Those who aspired to the position were obliged to ally with magnificoes beyond the county. Activists in Limerick most obviously enjoyed useful contacts with those high in government during the Tory heyday: first the general and lord justice, Sir Richard Ingoldsby, and then Lord Chancellor Phipps. By the same token, the Tories' shipwreck cast locals adrift. Yet, in that spirit of adaptation which helped so many of the quondam Tories to survive and even reappear in the Dublin parliament of 1727, fresh alliances were constructed. By the 1740s the new lord chancellor Jocelyn, future Lord Newport and earl of Roden, interested himself in what was going on in Limerick, where he had personal and professional contacts.[7] Smythe and Hasset were strategically placed to enlist others important in government, the law and parliament. Nevertheless, despite these multifarious connections, it was the Massys who triumphed. So far, in explaining why Massy escaped punishment, much has been made of the local might of his family. This, together with the more general ambivalence of the authorities towards the act of abduction, might suffice to explain why Massy went free. The Massys were not as their enemies contended. Already, doubts have been raised as to whether they were as wild and savage as their denigrators claimed. Nor should it be supposed that the Massys were totally cut off from the influential in Dublin. In the Southwells they possessed patrons who, intermittently, were heeded in the capital. Dean Massy, whose education had been at Dublin University, retained acquaintances there. Moreover, those to whom the dean appealed in the locality to assist his campaign against the corrupt oligarchy in Limerick included the Burtons of Buncraggy: a dynasty, thanks to its origins and marriages intimate with the Donegal mafia, which, headed by the Conollys, still counted for much in government circles.[8] At least by tradition, the Southwells also moved in the same orbit.

Other factors meant that the events in Limerick might alarm the authorities in Dublin and oblige them to investigate what had been happening there. The denouement of the Ingoldsby affair coincided with a time of heightened anxiety. By 1744 domestic and international dangers loomed. Coastal districts and inaccessible hills, a perennial worry to the authorities, were now suspected of harbouring those who in an emergency might betray Protestant Ireland. Fears lest the disaffected Irish be recruited in greater numbers to fight for Britain's enemies or that those already marching under French colours would now return to Ireland stimulated greater vigilance.[9] The jumpy might have interpreted the depredations of Massy, and his sudden voyages to and from Bordeaux, as a cover for nefarious schemes. In addition, the presence among his gang of several whose names spoke of Irish Catholic lineage and affiliations invested the raid on Nantenan with ominous meanings. Notwithstanding these worries, Massy was never cast as even a possible rebel. The topical Jacobite scares were not used to blacken him. During the case, when reference was made to the Stuarts, it was to their earlier history and then probably ironically. After Frances Massy landed at Limerick in 1744, it was noted that she was pregnant. One wag observed that it was lucky that the couple had stayed away fewer than nine months, 'otherwise perhaps we should have had a pretender cried up'.[10] When the child, a daughter, was born, it was remarked sardonically that 'no prince's birth was ever attended with more witnesses'.[11] Only a handy fortune, not, as in the warming-pan scandal of 1688, a kingdom, was at stake. The Massys' opponents may have refrained from making political capital from the confessional and possible political leanings of the kidnappers because they themselves were vulnerable to comparable accusations. Jack Williams, as we have seen, by communion and blood was part of Catholic Ireland. Had the Massys and Southwells chosen to do so, the now spectral Toryism of the Ingoldsby-Smythe-Hasset connection could easily be traced back to the more full-blooded and embarrassing variety of Queen Anne's time.

The motive behind Hugh Massy's grabbing of Frances Ingoldsby, dis-
counting simple lust, seems to have been his need dramatically to improve his
own straitened circumstances. This crime, like so many other abductions, arose
from the grim social and economic prospects for cadets within the rapidly
growing landed order. Landowners worked ruthlessly, whether in parliament
or their localities, to protect and enlarge their holdings. However, for those
such as Hugh Fitzjohn Massy, consigned by birth to the precarious fringes of
that privileged society, concern for his livelihood was inseparable from worry
over his standing. Those born into the landed gentry but without the where-
withal to continue to live as such willingly tried alternative careers. Massy's
own description as an attorney suggests the route he was taking for financial
survival. Apprehensions were not all economic. Being accounted a gentleman
carried intangible benefits. Any danger of derogation threatened reputation
and the sense of honour. This same obsession with honour, it has been argued
recently, needs to be incorporated into accounts of political behaviour.[12] A quest
for honour may run through the taking of Frances Ingoldsby, the Massys'
determined defence of their beleaguered member and the preoccupations of
members of parliament.

Those who skirmished in the houses of parliament or duelled at dawn spoke
the languages of honour.[13] It has been implied sometimes that the definition
of what constituted honourable conduct was agreed among the gentlemen of
eighteenth-century Ireland. But, on the contrary, contemporaries wrangled
over the term. Indeed eighteenth-century commentators were less starry-eyed
than some later analysts. Scripture and classical texts guided the uncertain
towards correct notions of honour; heralds and other pundits also proffered
vade-mecums. Contingent, mutable, disputed: like other forms of right conduct,
honour was so variously defined as to bewilder. One astringent writer in the
Ireland of the 1760s decried the prevailing but false ideas of honour, which
'are the greatest depravities of human nature, by giving wrong ambitions and
false ideas of what is good and laudable'.[14] Closer to the setting of the Limerick
controversy, in 1751 a political aspirant complained that 'the word *honour* is too
often a prostitute to the vilest purposes; in short it is no longer binding than
it is useful to the prosecution of men's worldly interests'.[15]

These eighteenth-century cynics need not destroy the possibility that the
actors in the Ingoldsby affair were motivated by a wish to enhance or vindicate
their honour. Even so the sceptics should warn against trusting too readily the
professions of those who insisted that their behaviour, when apparently self-
regarding or self-indulgent, was inspired by honour. What hampers the use of
honour to unlock some of the mysteries of the Ingoldsby legend is the
absence of any mention of it in the voluminous documentation which the
case generated. Again, this lack, although noteworthy, is not surprising. In the
nature of the testimony assembled to back the legal argument, facts – who did

what, and where and when – not intangibles were of the greatest moment. An unspoken anxiety over reputation and by implication with honour may nevertheless be concealed behind the formulaic utterances. Certainly, ideas of the fitting and unfitting recurred throughout the evidence. In particular, as has been emphasized, Frances Ingoldsby was represented as inverting the conventions of female decorum. In addition, the Massys, *en masse*, signified menace. It might be possible that this threat arose because, for their foes, they embodied archaic and discredited notions of honour; or that they themselves acted in accordance with a code in which ambush and intimidation were legitimate tactics. Throughout eighteenth-century Ireland, as in most contemporary societies, violence was regarded ambivalently. On occasion it enhanced rather than tarnished the reputation of the violent. Paradoxically, the victim, such as the pitiable Frances Ingoldsby, was the more dishonoured. Ideas of honour could with ingenuity be read into the incident, as into the activities of parliament-men. Even so, it is striking that neither side in its many extant statements portrayed itself as actuated by honour. Instead, with startling candour each acknowledged how it contended for power and property.

The want of any apologia based on honour makes it harder to link the dynamics of the local with the febrile but supposedly principled politics of the centre. In Limerick itself, the Whiggish officers of the garrison who mocked the Tory Bishop Smythe in 1710; the civic notables who protested against the wiles of Pearce and Ingoldsby in 1727; Charles Massy as he pilloried venal functionaries in the corporation; and Edmund Sexten Pery when he knit together the interests of locale and kingdom into a brand of patriotism: all insisted that their principles lifted them high above their shabbily unprincipled opponents. In the same manner, the confederacy of Smythe, Hasset and Maunsell asserted an ethical superiority over its rivals. It implied a better respect for the law, and the property which it safeguarded. But if a significant principle lurked here – regard for the rule of law – it was never fully expounded. Moreover, as has been demonstrated, the law was used simply as a tool the value of which was set by its speed and efficiency in dealing with the controverted matters. Accordingly, a brutal pragmatism characterized both plaintiffs and defendants in this case. Arguably a similar pragmatism marked local and national politics. Sometimes it was concealed – and simultaneously forwarded – behind a vocabulary of liberty, public interest and patriotism. These terms degenerated into parroted lessons, with few, whether servants of the court or staunch independents, willing to allow others to monopolize claims to patriotism and civic virtue. In 1756 Judge Michael Ward mordantly reflected how during his lengthy career the cant phraseology of politicians had slipped from one timely slogan to the next. 'The Patriot alias Protestant alias Whig interest', he concluded unexceptionably, 'must be the natural interest of Ireland'.[16] Through tone and timbre, gesture and stance, auditors and onlookers might distinguish the true alloy from the base. Modern historians, denied such aids, if they assess the roles of honour and principle, are left with imponderables about motives and sincerity which at this distance can only be guessed.

More appropriately perhaps, given the skills of historians, shifts in terminology and usage can be tracked. In particular, the concept of 'interest' awaits more minute scrutiny. Interest described both the concrete, as in the assertion of a proprietor's claims to nominate members of parliament and corporations in his bailiwick. It could also be applied to larger and abstract entities, notably the Protestant Interest, which often comprehended the entire system of legal and social privilege erected between the early seventeenth and early eighteenth centuries.[17] The duties of property-owning conventionally included upholding the interest, not just of the owner's family, but of the estate, its tenants and of the surrounding parish, barony or county. In obeying these imperatives, the active fused and so confused the public and private interests. Under cover of a lofty public-spiritedness, it often seemed as if material self-interests benefited most. The doctrine and practice of civic activism lay at the heart of eighteenth-century politics. If it encouraged participation in the deliberations of the national senate, it valued other activities in the public sphere. The historians of high politics, in focussing on the few dramatic confrontations on College Green, have ignored the tedious routines more characteristic of the experience of an assiduous member of parliament. Moreover, those elected to the house regarded it as merely one among many calls on their time when in Dublin, and seldom the most pressing. Absenteeism was rife. Often members were content to pursue their objectives, whether public or private, in a variety of places, of which again the Parliament House was but one, alongside Dublin Castle, the Customs House, Barrack and Linen Boards or county assizes and sessions. For the majority of the politically active, membership of these several bodies arose naturally from their position as substantial owners of property. As these busy squires rode from court house to tavern, masonic lodge to assembly room, smart Dublin drum to tedious committee, they did not, unlike some modern historians, compartmentalize their different endeavours. In the same way, the local excitements generated yearly by celebrations and processions were supplemented by episodic elections or by occasional public wrangles like that over Frances Ingoldsby. The abduction of the heiress may have originated as an impulsive act by one man, but soon enough its ramifications turned it into public spectacle. As such, it furnished the latest test for those alliances which had for so long fought to control Limerick and its environs: a fight at once ritualized and in deadly earnest. It did not decide the campaign, but the outcome showed how the balance of local power was tilting away from the old Ingoldsby grouping and towards the Massys.

The rancour of eighteenth-century Irish politics excited frequent comment. In parliament itself, the temptation to elevate the epic at the expense of the humdrum may again stress combat and ignore consensus. In the localities, the placid similarly attracts little notice. Elections notoriously offered evidence of frenzied activity, highly personalized rivalries and open corruption. The ferocity with which the 1761 contest for Kerry had been fought led one local to lament that 'the spirit of party and faction predominates'.[18] Efforts to apportion the seats amicably broke down because old feuds, even hatreds, were too intense. Simply to transpose the rivalries in a neighbouring county into Limerick would be unwarranted. Even so, some of the factors which turned Kerry into a battle-ground – such as sharp geographical divisions which allowed notables to dominate their immediate district but not the whole county – recurred in Limerick. In its own right, and not as a pallid mirror of excitements elsewhere, Limerick possessed its own long history of polarized politics. After the burst of electioneering between 1692 and 1713, the Hanoverian succession and the installation of a Whig oligarchy might have calmed the scene. Now only the death of the sovereign triggered general elections: in 1715, 1727 and 1761. Vacancies through death or the elevation of a sitting member to the peerage (in Limerick, usually a Southwell) or to the judicial bench (as happened at Tralee in Kerry with Arthur Hasset in 1743) brought less predictable competitions. By-elections for the county of Limerick were held in 1716, 1721, 1729 and 1759; and for the city in 1731, 1739 and 1741.

The naive supposed that these elections disrupted local harmony. Not only did they invent a harmony which had rarely existed; they mistook symptom for cause. Elections brought into the open animosities which already ran through the political community. On occasion they could add fresh grievances, with promises seemingly broken, slights given and taken or ancient alliances disregarded, but seldom created enmities *ab initio*. The long drawn out contentions over Frances Ingoldsby had the same effect. They exposed to view the divisions which, it was well known, seamed Protestant society in Limerick and the surrounding counties. Additional and unusual evidence of those tensions is afforded by a unique survival. One of the most arresting images of the denizens of early eighteenth-century Ireland portrays the initiates of the Limerick Hell Fire Club.[19] Painted about 1736, the group portrait commemorates thirteen men and one woman. The painting is not without its puzzles, including the identities of those whom it includes. At least two of those in it would soon be conspicuous in the Ingoldsby chronicle: Hasset or Blennerhasset of Riddlestown and Royse of Nantenan. Accordingly it conjures up much of the ambience in which the orphaned Frances Ingoldsby found herself. It also shows the society of her keepers, not of her abductors, the Massys. The company is engaged neither in war nor sport, but in conviviality and conversation. Smart adjuncts of sociability are displayed. The sitters wear fashionable waistcoats, surcoats, cravats and wigs. They pose around a table, with elaborate chairs, decanters, glasses, punch bowl and wine cooler, all of which announce their power and style as consumers. In some of their later propaganda, members of the circle wished to deny this polish to the Massys. The

8. Limerick Hell Fire Club, *c.* 1736.
(courtesy of National Gallery of Ireland)

singularity of the canvas is increased, indeed lifted onto another plane, by the presence of the solitary woman. Thanks to her posture, with one hand clasped by a man while a second paws her and beckons, it emits an electric charge. Whoever she is – Arthur Hasset's wife has been proposed[20] – she catches the lubricious atmosphere which may have enveloped Riddlestown and Nantenan. It may be fanciful, but the unabashed gaze of the woman encapsulates the predicament of Frances Ingoldsby: at once in danger and a danger.

A segment of Limerick's notables met together regularly and thought of themselves as enough of a group to merit the collective portrait. The circle was not exactly coterminous with the alliance which oversaw Frances Ingoldsby and later confronted the Massys. The club included settlers of different vintages and was not confined to the arbitrary boundaries of County Limerick. As such it hinted at the adventitious ways in which social gatherings were composed: of those who shared tastes, kinship, neighbourhood or philosophies. Cells of this kind, sometimes overlapping in membership, at other times discrete, composed the elites of Protestant Ireland. Terrain played a part. The inhabitants of one province tended to herd together with one another against those from the others. Town might be ranged against countryside; mountain-dwellers against lowlanders. Since the sixteenth century rivalries had been noted between people 'of the mountains, valley and seacoasts'.[21] Such tensions re-appeared in the fracas over Frances Ingoldsby. But in the end, while propinquity and shared habits united members of the same kindred and locality, they could be transcended by more personal factors. So much was shown by the associates in the Hell Fire Club, and again in the groupings which squared up to one another over the fate of the heiress. Common backgrounds, privileges and confession could encourage cooperation. Yet these same influences had created vendettas, both personal and ideological, and competition for local and national power. The vicious struggle over Frances Ingoldsby suggests how these forces continued to disturb provincial Ireland, and so divided the Protestant interest.

Notes

B.L.   British Library, London
N.A.   National Archives, Dublin
N.L.I.   National Library of Ireland, Dublin
P.R.O.N.I.   Public Record Office of Northern Ireland, Belfast
Rathkeale   Palatine Museum, Rathkeale, Co. Limerick
R.C.B.   Representative Church Body Library, Dublin
R.D.   Registry of Deeds, Dublin

ABDUCTIONS

1 J. Ingram to W. Smythe, 10 May 1744 (N.L.I., PC 445).
2 Rental of Ingoldsby lands, 1741–42; rental, 1757 (N.L.I., PC 438).
3 J.A. Froude, *The English in Ireland*, (3 vols, London 1881), i, pp 464–82.
4 W.E.H. Lecky, *Ireland in the eighteenth century* (5 vols, London 1892), i, pp 373–89.
5 G.E. Howard, *Queries relative to the several defects and grievances in some of the present laws of Ireland*, 2nd edn. (Dublin 1761), pp 19–20.
6 J. Kelly, 'The abduction of women of fortune in eighteenth-century Ireland' in *Eighteenth-Century Ireland* 9 (1994), pp 7–43.
7 Kelly, 'Abduction of women', pp 41–3. On the social and economic conditions, both generally and in the most affected counties: J. Burtchaell and D. Dowling, 'Social and economic conflict in County Kilkenny, 1600–1800' in K. Whelan and W. Nolan (eds) *Kilkenny: History and Society* (Dublin 1990), pp 256–66; L.M. Cullen, *The emergence of modern Ireland 1600–1900* (London 1981); D. Dickson, 'An economic

history of the Cork region in the eighteenth century' (unpublished Ph.D. thesis, Trinity College Dublin, 1977); T.P. Power, *Land, politics and society in eighteenth-century Tipperary* Oxford 1993).
8 12 Geo I, *c*.iii; 9 Geo II, *c*.xi; 19 Geo II, *c*.xiii; 23 Geo II, *c*.x.
9 This episode is treated in J. Cunningham, *A history of Castle Caldwell and its families* (Monaghan *c*.1980), pp 65–8; D. Boyle, *Half-hanged McNaghten* (Derry 1993); Kelly, 'Abduction of women', pp 26–7.
10 The classic exposition of the concept is K.V. Thomas, 'The double-standard' in *Journal of the History of Ideas* 20 (1959).
11 W. Crofts to Lord Perceval, 15 July 1743 , 20 May 1746 (B.L., Additional Ms. 47009A, ff. 144, 181).
12 R. Purcell to Lord Perceval, 24 June 1746 (B.L., Additional Ms. 47002A, f.46).
13 The fundamental reassessment of this group remains D. Dickson, 'Middlemen' in T. Bartlett and D.W. Hayton (eds) *Penal era and Golden age* (Belfast 1979), pp 162–85. For other discussions: K. Whelan, 'An underground gentry? Catholic

middlemen in eighteenth-century
Ireland' in *Eighteenth-Century Ireland*
10 (1995), reprinted in K. Whelan,
The tree of liberty (Cork 1996), pp 3–
56; T.C. Barnard, 'The gentrification
of eighteenth-century Ireland' in
Eighteenth-Century Ireland 12 (1997).
14 The collection is now in N.L.I., PC
434–449. Some indication of its
scope is offered by S.R. Penny,
*Smythe of Barbavilla: the history of an
Anglo-Irish family* (Oxford 1974).
15 Powerful recent accounts include:
S.J. Connolly, *Religion, law and power:
the making of Protestant Ireland 1660–
1760* (Oxford 1992); P. McNally,
'The Hanoverian accession and the
Tory party in Ireland' in *Parliamentary
History* 14 (1995), pp 263–83;
McNally, *Parties, patriots and under-
takers:parliamentary politics in early
Hanoverian Ireland* (Dublin 1997).
These build on rather than super-
sede the pioneering analyses by
D.W. Hayton: 'Ireland and the
English ministers, 1707–1716'
(unpublished D.Phil. thesis, Oxford
University, 1975); 'The beginnings
of the "Undertaker System"' in
Bartlett and Hayton (eds) *Penal era
and golden age*; 'Walpole and Ireland'
in J. Black (ed) *Britain in the age of
Walpole* (London 1984).
16 A.P.W. Malcomson, ''The
parliamentary traffic of this country'
in Bartlett and Hayton (eds), *Penal
era and golden age*.
17 P. O'Connor, *Exploring Limerick's
history* (Coolanoran 1987).
18 *Abstract of the number of protestant and
popish families . . . in the years 1732
and 1733* (Dublin 1736).
19 D. Dickson, '"Centres of motion":
Irish cities and the origins of
popular politics' in L. Bergeron and
L.M. Cullen (eds) *Culture et pratiques
politiques en France et en Irlande,
XVIe–XVIIIe siecle* (Paris 1990),
p. 106.

20 Autobiography of Joseph Wight, 20
June 1752, 31 March 1753 (Friends'
Historical Library, Dublin): P.M.
Kerrigan, *Castles and fortifications in
Ireland, 1485–1945* (Cork 1995), pp
134–5, 140.
21 A.J. Guy, 'The Irish military establishment, 1660–1776' in T. Bartlett
and K. Jeffery (eds) *A military history
of Ireland* (Cambridge 1996), p. 220;
T.C. Barnard, 'Integration or
separation? Hospitality and display
in Protestant Ireland, 1660–1800' in
L.W.B. Brockliss and D.S. Eastwood
(eds), *A union of multiple identities: the
British Isles, c.1750–1850* (Manchester
1997), p. 138.
22 Autobiography of J.A. Oughton
(National Army Museum, London,
Ms. 8008–36–1, p. 61); Autobiography
of Joseph Wight, 8, 22, 23, 24 May
1752, 11 June 1752, 12, 14, 18 May
1753 (Friends' Historical Library,
Dublin).
23 T.C. Barnard, 'Athlone, 1685;
Limerick, 1710: religious riots or
charivaris?' in *Studia Hibernica* 27
(1993), pp 71–5.
24 Brown family history (Rathkeale,
Southwell-Brown Mss.); thanks-
giving sermons by Rev. Stacpole
Pery (?) (N.L.I., Ms. 16094).
25 Journal of Nicholas Peacock, 1
March 1743[4], 25 Nov. 1744
(N.L.I., Ms. 16091).
26 Journal of Lucas 14 Jan. 1740[1], 9,
10 June 1741 (N.L.I., MS. 14101);
Journal of Peacock, *passim* (N.L.I.,
Ms. 16091); Autobiography of
Wight, 12, 19 May 1753 (Friends'
Historical Library, Dublin).
27 Merchant's ledger of Limerick
(N.L.I., Ms. 827); J. Brady, *Catholics
and catholicism in the eighteenth-century
press* (Maynooth 1965), p. 74.
28 *A true state of the present affairs of
Limerick* (London 1726); M.
Lenihan, *Limerick: its history and
antiquities* (Dublin 1866), p. 340;

C. Massy, *A collection of resolutions, queries, &c. wrote on the occasion of the present dispute in the city of Limerick* (Limerick 1769); E. O'Flaherty, 'Urban politics and municipal reform in Limerick, 1723–62' in *Eighteenth-Century Ireland* 6 (1991), pp 112–19.

29 T.C. Barnard, *Cromwellian Ireland* (Oxford 1975), p. 65

30 T.C. Barnard, 'Settling and unsettling Ireland; the Cromwellian and Williamite revolutions' in J.H. Ohlmeyer (ed), *Ireland from independence to occupation* (Cambridge 1995), p. 274.

31 *Richard Pococke's Irish Tours*, ed. J. McVeagh (Dublin 1995), p. 97.

32 Autobiography of Joseph Wight, 18 May 1752 (Friends' Historical Library, Dublin).

33 Minute book of the Limerick guild of masons, 1747–57, 24 May 1755 (Limerick Civic Museum).

34 Massy, *Collection of resolutions*.

35 Poll books for 1731 and 1761 (B.L., Additional Ms. 31888; N.L.I., Mss. 16092, 16093).

36 J.L. McCracken, 'Irish parliamentary elections, 1727–68' in *Irish Historical Studies* v (1947), pp 209–30.

37 D.W. Hayton, 'Ireland and the English ministers'; D.W. Hayton, 'The crisis in Ireland and the disintegration of Queen Anne's last ministry' in *Irish Historical Studies* xxii (1981), pp 193–215.

38 D.W. Hayton, *Ireland after the Glorious Revolution* (Belfast 1976); Hayton, 'Walpole and Ireland'; Hayton, 'The beginnings of the "Undertaker System"; Hayton (and D. Szechi), John Bull's other kingdoms' in C. Jones (ed.), *Britain in the first age of party 1680–1750* (London 1987), pp 259–79.

INGOLDSBYS AND MASSYS

1 Case of John Bourcher (N.L.I., PC 445); J. Ingram to W. Smythe, 15 Nov. 1743 (N.L.I., PC 445).

2 C.H. Firth and G. Davies, *The regimental history of Cromwell's Army* (2 vols, Oxford 1940), ii, pp 644–7.

3 On the Waller connection: A. Clarke, *The Old English in Ireland, 1625–42* (London 1966), p. 135; Firth and Davies, *Regimental history*, ii, pp 442–8; M. MacCarthy-Morrogh, *The Munster plantation: English migration to southern Ireland 1583–1641* (Oxford 1986), pp 245, 263.

4 Release of lands from Sir Richard Ingoldsby to Sir George Ingoldsby, 15 Dec. 1668 (N.L.I., PC 349, box 2); S. Pender (ed.) *A 'census' of Ireland, c.1659* (Dublin 1939), p. 275.

5 Corporation book of Limerick (B.L., Additional Ms. 19859, f.3v); Order by commissioners of act of settlement, 19 Nov. 1663 (N.L.I., PC 877, envelope 33); Barnard, *Cromwellian Ireland*, p. 65; Firth and Davies, *Regimental history*, ii, p. 646; G.E.C., *Complete baronetage* (6 vols, London 1900–9), iii, p. 228; R.C. Simington (ed), *The Civil Survey, AD 1654–1656*. iv *County of Limerick* (Dublin 1938), pp 77, 79, 85, 106, 274, 285–6, 327, 442, 472, 478, 482.

6 Limerick rentals (Houghton Library, Harvard University, Orrery Mss, Ms. 218 22F); Samuel Foxon to Orrery, 1 April 1667 (op. cit.); Orrery to S. Creagh (draft), 26 Feb. 1677[8] (Petworth House, West Sussex, Orrery Mss., general series, 29); G. Fitzgerald to Orrery, 12 Jan. 1678[[9] (op. cit.); J. Hall to Orrery, 14 Dec. 1669 (ibid., general series, 28); Lord O'Brien to Orrery, 22 July 1670 (op. cit.); Orrery to Lord Lieutenant and Council, 23 Sep. 1670 (op. cit.); brief of Orrery's affairs, 17 July 1676

(ibid., general series, 17); Orrery to Sir R. Southwell, 21 May 1672 (Victoria and Albert Museum, Orrery letters, i, f. 13); list of Roman Catholic freemen admitted to Limerick, 1672 (ibid., i, f. 37); T.C. Barnard, 'The political, material and mental culture of the Cork settlers, c.1649–1700' in P. O'Flanagan and C.G. Buttimer (eds), *Cork: History and Society* (Dublin 1993), pp 319–21.

7   Diary of Bishop Simon Digby, 1688–9 (Lambeth Palace Library, Ms. 3152, ff. 20–1, 29v); Sir T. Southwell to Lord Coningsby, 5 Aug. 1697, 22 Oct. 1697, 28 Oct. 1701, 21 Sep. 1705, 29 April 1707 (P.R.O.N.I., D 638/1/1, 3, 6, 18, 20, 21); Sir R. Cox to E. Southwell, 22 Dec. 1705 (B.L., Additional Ms. 38153, f. 128); B. Taylor to Lord Perceval, 21 Jan. 1714[15] (B.L., Additional Ms. 46966, f. 14); *Hibernia's lamentation: an elegyac poem; occasioned by the much lamented death of . . . Thomas Southwell* (Dublin 1720); P. McNally, 'Patronage and politics in Ireland, 1714–1727', (Unpublished Ph.D. thesis, Queen's University, Belfast, 1993), p. 99; McNally, *Parties, patriots and undertakers*, p. 106.

8   T. Southwell to J. Brown, 28 May 1761, 24 Aug. 1762, 19 Feb. 1763, 14 March 1763 (Rathkeale, Southwell-Brown Mss., box 1, bundle 2); T.C. Barnard, 'Protestantism, ethnicity and Irish identities, 1660–1760' in A. Claydon and I. McBride (eds) *Chosen Peoples* (Cambridge 1998): G.E.C., *The complete peerage* (12 vols, London 1910–59) xii, pt. 1, pp 148–9; P. O'Connor, *All Ireland is in and about Rathkeale* (Coolanoran 1996), p. 96–9.

9   W. Burne to W. Smythe, 14 Feb. 1711 [12] (N.L.I., PC 445); will of Lt. Gen. R. Ingoldsby, (P.R.O.N.I., T.808, p. 11615); Historic Manuscripts Commission, *Portland Mss.* v, p. 102;

Historic Manuscripts Commission, *16th Report, Mrs Frankland-Russell-Astley*, p. 203; *The form of the proceeding to the funeral of Lieutenant General Ingoldsby* (Dublin 1711/12).

10   A. Horner, 'Carton, Co. Kildare: a case study of the making of an Irish demesne' in *Quarterly Bulletin of the Irish Georgian Society* xviii (1975), p. 50; Lord Walter Fitzgerald, 'Carton' in *Journal of the County Kildare Archaeological Society* iv (1903–5), p. 12. For the house's appearance at this time, see J. Harris, *The artist and the country house* revised edn. (London 1985), plate 161.

11   *A catalogue of the household goods, of the late Henry Ingoldsby . . . to be sold by auction in Mary's Street . . . the 29th day of November 1731* (Dublin 1731); *A catalogue of the china ware and linnen of the late Henry Ingoldsby . . . to be sold by auction at his late house in Mary's Street . . . the 8th day of December, 1731* (Dublin 1731).

12   Penny, *Smythes of Barbavilla*, pp 37–48.

13   A. Blennerhasset to W. Smythe, 5 Feb. 1736[7], 12 June 1737 (N.L.I., PC 448); same to R. Jocelyn, 16 Sep. 1737 (P.R.O.N.I., Roden Mss., microfilm 147); genealogy of the Blennerhassets (P.R.O.N.I. D 680/3/1, p. 6); R.D., 81/109/56350; F.E. Ball, *The judges in Ireland 1221–1921* (2 vols, London 1926), ii, pp 207–8; E. Keane, P.B. Phair and T.U. Sadleir (eds), *King's Inns admission papers 1607–1867* (Dublin 1982), p. 41.

14   List of Irish parliament, 1713 (B.L., Additional Ms. 61637A); Viscount Gort, history of the Gort family, pp 214–17 (Glin Castle, Co. Limerick), Lenihan confused 'son' with 'son-in-law' and so invented 'Ingoldsby Phipps': *Limerick*, p. 316.

15   Account of Limerick property, 1 May 1730 (N.L.I., PC 438); H. Ingoldsby to W. Smythe, 3 May 1730 (N.L.I., PC445). Higgins was also a

tenant to some of the Limerick property of the Ingoldsbys: R.D., 23/65/12633; 41/37/24364; 54/370/36100.

16 W. Burne to W. Smythe, 26 Feb. 1711[12] (N.L.I., PC 445); will of Ingoldsby (P.R.O.N.I., T.808, p. 11615).

17 W. Burne to William Smythe, 1 Dec. 1711 (N.L.I., PC 445); W. Perceval to A. Charlet, 1 Nov. 1711 (Bodleian Library, Oxford, Ballard Ms. 36, f.70); J. Coughlan to T. Baker, 20 Nov. 1711 (N.L.I., Ms. 13242).

18 Hayton, 'Crisis in Ireland'. Phipps had visited Limerick in 1711: Bishop T. Lindsay to A. Charlet, 13 April 1711 (Bodleian Library, Oxford, Ballard Ms.8, f.90).

19 Petition of Francis Higgins (ibid., Ms. North A.3, f.237) (I owe this reference to Dr. David Hayton); D.W. Hayton, 'The high church party in the Irish Convocation, 1703–1713', forthcoming; *A letter to Mr. H-gg-s, from a student in the university* (Dublin 1718).

20 History of the Gort family, p. 217 (Glin Castle, Co. Limerick); Barnard, 'Athlone, 1685; Limerick, 1710', pp 71–4.

21 W. Perceval to A. Charlet, 20 Nov. 1718 (Bodleian Library, Oxford, Ballard Ms. 36, f.107); N.A., Calendar of Presentments, (Limerick), Jan. 1724[5]; *A true state*, pp 12, 47, 52.

22 H. Ingoldsby to W. Smythe, 3 April 1716, 30 March 1716[17] (N.L.I., PC 445).

23 List of Parliament men, 1713 (B.L., Additional Ms. 61637A).

24 H. Ingoldsby to W. Smythe, 30 July 1720, 18 Jan. 1723[4], 22 Jan 1723[4], 8 Feb. 1723[4] (N.L.I., PC 445).

25 Same to same, 3 April 1716 (op. cit.)

26 History of the Brown family (Rathkeale, Southwell-Brown Mss.); *A true state*.

27 J. Smythe to W. Smythe, 8 Feb. 1727[8] (N.L.I., PC 449); *A true state*, p. 19. In 1719 Ingoldsby's Dublin house had been searched for evidence of his links with the exiled Jacobite Duke of Ormonde: Abp. Lindsay of Armagh to A. Charlet, 31 Jan. 1718[19] (Bodleian Library, Oxford, Ballard Ms. 8, f. 113v).

28 H. Ingoldsby to W. Smythe, 6 Sep. 1725, 3 May 1730 (N.L.I., PC 445).

29 A. Blennerhasset to W. Smythe, 8 June 1734, 26 Dec. 1738 (N.L.I., PC 448).

30 O. Crofton to F. Ingoldsby, 16 June 1733 and undated (N.L.I., PC 436); F. Ingoldsby to O. Crofton, 21 Dec. 1734 (op. cit.); J. Wilde to W. Smythe, 11 Aug. 1733 (N.L.I., PC 449); A. Blennerhasset to same, 16 Aug. 1733 (N.L.I., PC 448).

31 Will of H. Ingoldsby, 24 July 1731, with codicil, 28 July 1731 (N.L.I., PC 438). A copy is in R.D., 94/361/66698.

32 James Smythe to W. Smythe, 10 March 1733[4] (N.L.I., PC 449).

33 J.L. Napper to same, 14 March 1733[4] (N.L.I., PC 436): fee book of J. Pickard, pp. 21v–2, 23, 52v (Dorset County Record Office, D/BLX, B5); account book of J. Pickard, ff. 109, 110, 118–18v (ibid., D/BLX, B1).

34 Copy of will of Sir John Dutton, 30 March 1742 (Gloucestershire County Record Office, D 678).

35 R. Smythe to J. Bonnell, 27 Dec. 1743 (N.L.I., PC 435); 'Case of Ralph Smythe and T.H. Royse' [1774] (N.L.I., PC 438); case papers, 1777 (op. cit.); 'Case of John Napper, a minor', 30 Oct. 1755 (op. cit.); J. Williams to ?W. Smythe, 13 Nov. 1750 (N.L.I., PC 447); undated letter of J. Williams to R. Smythe (op. cit.).

36 *A catalogue of the household goods; A catalogue of the china ware*; E. Butler

to W. Smythe, 7 July 1735 (N.L.I., PC 449); *Records of eighteenth-century domestic architecture in Dublin* (5 vols, Dublin 1912), iv, pp 39–40.

37 James Smythe to W. Smythe, 17 March 1731[2], 31 March 1732 (N.L.I., PC 449); J.L. Napper to same, 27 Aug. 1737, 19 March 1738[9] (N.L.I., PC 436); R. French to same, 18 Nov. 1738 (N.L.I., PC 449); Horner, 'Carton', pp 55, 60, 62; Fitzgerald, 'Carton', p. 12.

38 A Blennerhasset to W. Smythe, 11 Nov. 1738, 11 Dec. 1738 (N.L.I., PC 448).

39 Affidavit of A. Blennerhasset, 21 Sep. 1743 (N.L.I., PC 438). Further evidence of co-operation between the two is in R.D., 123/409/85163.

40 J. Williams to R. Smythe, undated (N.L.I., PC 447).

41 Will of H. Ingoldsby, 1731 (N.L.I., PC 438).

42 Deposition of Margaret Purdon, 1755; case of John Napper, 1755 (op. cit.).

43 J. Williams to W. Smythe, 27 Sep. 1744 (N.L.I., PC 447); case of John Napper, 1755 (N.L.I., PC 438).

44 J. Williams to W. Smythe, 24 June 1743 (N.L.I., PC 447); R. Robinson to same, 16 July 1743 (N.L.I., PC 445).

45 Affidavits of Frances Ingoldsby, 14 Sep. 1743; William Crookshank, 16 Sep. 1743; R. Smythe [1777]; J. Williams [1777] (N.L.I., PC 438).

46 Crown entry books, Co. Dublin commissions of oyer and terminer, 1742–44, indictment 28, 5 April 1744 (N.A.); R. Robinson to W. Smythe, 16 July 1743 (N.L.I., PC 445).

47 Affidavit of J. Williams, 24 Aug. 1743 (N.L.I., PC 438); abstract of proceedings regarding the Williams–Ingoldsby marriage (N.L.I., PC 436). For Bindon, see D. Fitzgerald, Knight of Glin, "Francis Bindon, (c.1690–1765)' in *Quarterly Bulletiin of the Irish Georgian Society* x (1967),

p. 3; B. Ó Dálaigh, *Ennis in the eighteenth century:portrait of an urban community* (Dublin 1995), pp 40–1.

48 Crookshank had been mentioned in Ingoldsby's will in 1731 (N.L.I., PC 438). For further evidence of his long-standing involvement in the affiars of the family; affidavit of Crookshank, 16 Sep. 1743 (op. cit.); fee-book of J. Pickard, ff. 109, 110, 118–18v (Dorset County Record Office, D/BLX, B1); R.D. 94/361/66698.

49 Crown entry book, Co. Dublin, 1741–42 (N.A.); J. D'Alton, *The history of the county of Dublin* (Dublin 1838), p. 48.

50 Affidavits of Catherine Denny, 27 Aug. 1743; Frances Ingoldsby, 14 Sep. 1743; John Murphy, 14 Sep. 1743; W. Crookshank, 16 Sep. 1743; Alderman Burrows, 16 Sep. 1743 (N.L.I., PC 438).

51 Affidavit of J. Murphy, 14 Sep. 1743 (op. cit.).

52 J. Ingram to W. Smythe, 6 April 1744 (N.L.I., PC 445).

53 Case of John Bourcher (op. cit.); case papers, 1777 (N.L.I., PC 438); R.D., 88/233/62364; 88/524/63576.

54 Abstract of proceedings in the Williams–Ingoldsby miarriage (N.L.I., PC 436).

55 J. Ingram to W. Smythe, 7 Jan. 1743[4] (N.L.I., PC 445); same to same, 20 July 1744 (op. cit.); case of John Bourcher (op. cit.).

56 Robinson's notes on legal cases (Pearse Street Public Library, Dublin, Gilbert Mss 34, p. 113); J. Ingram to W. Smythe, 9 Sep. 1746 (N.L.I., PC 445).

57 J. Ingram to W. Smythe, 18 Nov. 1743 (op. cit.); J. Begley, *The diocese of Limerick from 1691 to the present time* (Dublin 1938), p. 44.

58 J. Ingram to W. Smythe, 15 & 18 Nov. 1743; T. Royse to same, 26 Nov. 1743; Mrs. A. Royse to same,

20 Dec. 1747, (N.L.I., PC 445). For the long establishment of the Royses in the district: Leslie's succession list for the diocese of Limerick, pp 123–4, 165, 167, 252, 258 (R.C.B., Ms 61/2/13); County Limerick commission of the peace, 1730 (N.A., M 2296); Askeaton corporation book (National Library of Wales) (I owe the last reference to the kindness of M.D. Evans).

59 F. Massy to W. Smythe, 16 Jan. 1743[4] (N.L.I., PC 436); deposition of Elin Butler (N.L.I., PC 438).

60 T. Royse to W. Smythe, 26 Nov. 1743 (N.L.I., PC 445); F. Massy to same, 16 Jan. 1743[4] (N.L.I., PC 436); B.F. Barton, *Some account of the family of Barton* (Dublin 1902), p. 46.

61 J. Ingram to W. Smythe, 6 April 1744 (N.L.I., PC 445). Abstract of proceedings in the Williams-Ingoldsby marriage (N.L.I., PC 436). J. Ingram to W. Smythe, 15 Nov. 1743 (N.L.I., PC 445).

62 Same to same, 18 & 22 Nov. 1743, 24 Dec. 1743 (op. cit.); J.L. Napper to same, 1 March 1743[4] (N.L.I., PC 436).

63 J. Ingram to W. Smythe, 24 Dec. 1743 (N.L.I., PC 445).

64 F. Massy to same, 16 Jan. 1743[4] (N.L.I., PC 436).

65 R. Maunsell to same, 18 May 1744 (N.L.I., PC 445).

66 J. Ingram to same, undated [? Aug 1744] (N.L.I., PC 445).

67 Same to same, 6 April 1744 (N.L.I., PC 445).

68 Same to same, 6 April 1744, 20 July 1744 (N.L.I., PC 445).

69 Same to same, 7 Jan. 1743[4] (N.L.I., PC 445).

70 Same to same, 7 Jan. 1743[4] (N.L.I., PC 445).

71 Same to same, 20 July 1744 (N.L.I., PC 445).

72 Case papers, (N.L.I., PC 438); J. Ingram to W. Smythe, 1 Aug. 1746 (N.L.I., PC 445); E. Hickie to J. Williams, 5 June 1750 (op. cit.); J. Williams to W. Smythe, 26 March 1754 (op. cit.).

73 Case papers (N.L.I., PC 438). For Tunnadine's involvement in the Ingoldsby property, see J. Ingram to W. Smythe, 31 March 1747 (N.L.I., PC 445).

74 Same to same, 20 Aug 1745 (N.L.I., PC 445); case of John Napper, 30 Oct. 1755 (N.L.I., PC 438).

75 J. Ingram to W. Smythe, undated [? Aug 1745] (N.L.I., PC 445). For the Yorkes in Limerick: Council book of the corporation of Limerick, f.51 (B.L., Additional Ms. 19859); Lenihan, *Limerick*, pp 703–4.

76 J. Ingram to W. Smythe, undated [? Aug 1745] (N.L.I., PC 445); Robinson's notes on cases (Pearse St. Library, Dublin, Gilbert Ms. 34, pp 113–14).

77 Case of John Napper, 30 Oct. 1755 (N.L.I., PC 438).

78 J. Ingram to W. Smythe, 11 Aug. 1747 (N.L.I., PC 445); Mrs. A. Royse to same, 20 Dec.1747 (op. cit.); M.J. Dore, 'Monumental inscriptions at Nantinan, Co. Limerick' in *The Irish Ancestor* xii (1980), p. 62.

79 Newspaper advertisement of 22 March 1744[5], and declaration of W. Smythe, 25 March 1745 (N.L.I., PC 438); memorandum of William Smythe, 16 Feb. 1744[5] (N.L.I., PC 449).

80 Will of H. Ingoldsby, 1731 (N.L.I., PC 438).

81 Robinson's notes on cases (Pearse St. Library, Dublin, Gilbert Ms. 34, p. 113); R.D., 131/474/89899; 152/1/100472; Poll book, city of Limerick, 1761 (N.L.I., Ms. 16092).

82 *Report of the commissioners appointed to inquire into the state of the fairs and markets in Ireland*, Parliamentary papers xli, 1852–3 (Dublin 1853), p. 91. Later maps of parts of the estate are in N.L.I., 16 F 13.

83 T. Royse to W. Smythe, 9 Sep. 1746 (N.L.I., PC 445).

84 Rathkeale Parish Register, s.d. 1755 (Regional Archives, Limerick).

85 J. Ingram to W. Smythe, 20 Aug. 1745 (N.L.I., PC 445); memorial tablet at Temple Molagga church, Co. Cork which records the son's date of birth as 1 Nov. 1749.

86 Williams to R. Smythe, 20 Sep. 1771 (N.L.I., PC 445); case papers, 12 Aug. 1777 (N.L.I., PC 438).

87 Lenihan, *Limerick*, p. 745.

88 Case of R. Smythe and T.H. Royse, with opinion of R. Tisdall, 9 Jan. 1776; case papers, 1774 and 12 Aug. 1777 (N.L.I., PC 438).

89 Manuscript notes on the Massys (Stoneville, Co. Limerick) (I am grateful to Hugh Massy for copies of these); *A genealogical account of the Massy family* (Dublin 1890), pp 195–6; G.E.C., *Complete peerage*, viii, p. 549.

90 J. Ingram to W. Smythe, 15 & 18 Nov. 1743 (N.L.I., PC 445); C. Musgrave to A. Mason, 5 Nov. 1758 (Dromana, Co. Waterford, Villiers-Stuart Mss., B/7/38).

91 Notes of the Massys (Stoneville, Co. Limerick); *Genealogical account of the Massy family*; G.E.C., *Complete peerage*, viii, p. 549; commission of the peace, Co. Limerick, 1730 (N.A., M 2296); grand jury petition, 18 March 1731[2](N.L.I., PC 875, envelope 5); trustees for repair of road, 2 Oct. 1756 (Rathkeale, Southwell-Brown Mss., box 2, bundle 18); Lenihan, *Limerick*, pp 743–5.

92 O. Gallagher to O. St. George, 14 Dec. 1727 (Public Record Office, London, C 110/46); *Genealogical account of the Massy family*, pp 195–6.

93 A recent sensitive discussion of law and lawlessness is N. Garnham, 'How violent was eighteenth-century Ireland?' in *Irish Historical Studies* xxx (1997), pp 377–92. See, too N. Garnham, *The courts, crime and the criminal law in Ireland, 1692–1760* (Dublin 1996); Connolly, *Religion, law and power*, pp 198–262.

94 Robinson's notes on legal cases (Pearse St. Library, Dublin, Gilbert Ms. 34, pp 113–14).

95 Case of John Bourcher; J. Ingram to W. Smythe, 7 Jan. 1743[4] (N.L.I., PC 445).

96 Case papers, 1777–8 (N.L.I., PC 438); R.D., 131/474/89899; *Dublin Hibernian Journal*, 8 Nov. 1775.

97 M. Scanlan to J. Brown, 28 Jan. 1759 (Rathkeale, Southwell-Brown Mss., box 1, bundle 4).

98 Deposition of M. Purdon (N.L.I., PC 438).

99 List of papers left by J. Williams with Edmund Fitzgerald, Knight of Glin, 25 June 1768 (N.L.I., PC 445); affidavit of J. Williams, 1777 (N.L.I., PC 438).

100 Will of J. Williams, 26 Sep. 1782 (N.L.I., PC 447).

PROVINCIAL LIVES

1 Affidavit of R. Smythe, 1777 (N.L.I., PC 438).

2 J. Williams to W. Smythe, 11 Aug. 1759 (N.L.I., PC 447).

3 Same to same, 21 Feb. 1759 (N.L.I., PC 447); R. Smythe to J. Williams, 5 Oct. 1771 (op. cit.).

4 J. Williams to W. Smythe, 14 July 1759 (N.L.I., PC 447). For Arthur Rochfort, Lord Belfield'a brother: L. Daly, *Titles* (Mullingar 1981), pp 48–67.

5 J. Williams to W. Smythe, 6 Nov. 1744 (N.L.I., PC 447); same to J. Cooley, 28 June 1760 (N.L.I., PC 445); same to R. Smythe, 20 Sep. 1771 (op. cit.); affidavit of J. Williams, 1777 (N.L.I., PC 438).

6 'Instructions of J. Williams to R. Smythe' after 1770 (N.L.I., PC 436); J. Williams to Richard

Fitzgerald, 22 March 1774 (op. cit.); draft letter of R. Smythe, 12 Dec. 1775 (N.L.I., PC 445); affidavit of J. Williams, 1777 (N.L.I., PC 438).

7   J. Williams to ?R. Smythe, 3 March 1776 (N.L.I., PC 447).

8   Same to same, 3 July 1777 (N.L.I., PC 447).

9   A.P.W. Malcomson, *The pursuit of the heiress: aristocratic marriage in Ireland, 1750–1820* (Belfast 1982).

10 Affidavit of R. Smythe, 1777 (N.L.I., PC 438).

11 Deposition of M. Purdon (N.L.I., PC 438).

12 Robinson's notes on legal cases (Pearse St. Library, Dublin, Gilbert Ms. 34, p. 114).

13 Testimony of Ann Nash, undated (N.L.I., PC 438).

14 B. Badham to ? H. Boyle, 7 Nov. 1731 (P.R.O.N.I., D/2707/A1/11/37); Crown entry books, county and city of Dublin, proceedings of 26 Oct. 1741; 25 Oct. 1742; 25 Oct. 1743; 22 Oct. 1747; 21 Oct. 1752 (N.A., Crown entry books, city and county of Dublin, 1741–52); A. Carpenter (ed), *Verse in English from eighteenth-century Ireland* (Cork 1998), p. 493.

15 Testimony of Ann Nash, undated (N.L.I., PC 438).

16 Affidavit of C. Quinn, undated, ?1743 (N.L.I., PC 438).

17 Deposition of S. Madden, 1766 (N.L.I., PC 438).

18 J. Digby to W. Smythe, 11 Sep. 1736 (N.L.I., PC 445).

19 Affidavit of J. Williams, 23 Aug. 1743; affidavit of F. Ingoldsby, 14 Sep. 1743 (N.L.I., PC 438); case of John Bourcher (N.L.I., PC 445).

20 Case papers, 1777 (N.L.I., PC 438); M. Royse to J. Brown, n.d. (Rathkeale, Southwell-Brown Mss., box 1, bundle 2); R.D., 88/233/62364; 88/524/63576.

21 Frances Ingoldsby to W. Smythe, 16 Jan. 1738[9] (N.L.I., PC 436).

22 J. Ingram to same, undated, ?Aug. 1745 (N.L.I., PC 445).

23 E. Ball to J. Howlin, 6 Nov. 1750, 18 July 1753, 12 July [?1761]; C. Houghton to J. Howlin, 24 Dec 1752 (N.A., M 2663).

24 F. Bellew to Lord Strafford, 28 June 1729, 17 July 1729 (B.L., Additional Ms. 22228, ff. 47–53v).

25 J. Ingram to W. Smythe, undated [?Aug. 1745] (N.L.I., PC 445); J. Williams to same, 31 Aug. 1744 (N.L.I., PC 447).

26 T. Royse to same, 14 July 1746 (N.L.I., PC 445).

27 Same to same, 9 Sep. 1746 (N.L.I., PC 445).

28 J. Ingram to same, 18 Nov. 1743 (N.L.I., PC 445); J. Williams to same, 31 Aug. 1744 (N.L.I., PC 447); same to R. Smythe, 20 Sep. 1771 (N.L.I., PC 445).

29 Case papers, 12 Aug. 1777 (N.L.I., PC 438).

30 Op. cit.

31 R. Gillespie, 'Lords and commons in the seventeenth century' in R. Gillespie and G. Moran (eds), *'A various country': essays in Mayo history* (Westport 1987), p. 49.

32 Lord Perceval to B. Taylor, 18 Aug. 1715, 17 Sep. 1715, 20 Sep. 1715, 6 Oct. 1715, 12 Nov. 1715; B. Taylor to Lord Perceval, 2 Sep. 1715, 9 Sep. 1715, 21 Oct. 1715, (B.L., Additional Ms. 46966, ff. 91, 97, 105, 106, 111v–112, 118, 120v, 123v); list of Earl of Egmont's independent troop, 8 May, 1744 (B.L., Additional Ms. 47001B, f.66); R. Purcell to Lord Perceval, 17 Sep. 1745, 11 Oct. 1745 (ibid., ff. 133, 154); same to same, 3 & 7 Jan. 1745[6], 7 March 1745[6], 5 Aug. 1745 (B.L., Additional Ms. 47002A, ff. 1, 7–8, 27, 57); letter of 6 Sep. 1745 (N.A., Calendar of departmental correspondence, 1741–59); account book of Wynnes of Haselwood, 1737–51, entries for

4, 5, 11 Jan., 1745[6], 19 April 1746
(N.L.I., Ms., 5780).

33 T.C. Barnard, 'Lawyers and the law
in later seventeenth-century Ireland'
in *Irish Historical Studies* xxviii
(1993), pp 368–72; Garnham, *Courts,
crime and the criminal law*, pp 126–31.

34 Presentments before William Massy,
1746 (N.A., Calendar of presentments, Limerick, pp 190–1); J. Ingram
to W. Smythe, 18 Nov. 1743 (N.L.I.,
PC 445).

35 Poll book, Limerick, 1731 (B.L.,
Additional Ms. 31888, f.49).

36 Poll book, Limerick, 1761 (N.L.I.,
Ms. 16092).

37 R. Louth to M. Louth, 3 June 1755
(Bodleian Library, Oxford, Ms. Eng.
Lett. C 572, f.38v); White's annals of
Limerick (N.L.I., Ms. 2714, p. 133);
D. Fitzgerald, Knight of Glin, 'Three
eighteenth-century letters of Lady
Theodosia Crosbie's' in *Journal of the
Kerry Archaeological and Historical
Society* 17 (1984), pp 76–8.

38 White's annals of Limerick (N.L.I.,
Ms. 2714, pp 134–5).

39 D. O'Sullivan, *Carolan: the life, times
and music of an Irish harper* (2 vols,
London 1958), i, p. 112.

40 Massy, *Collection of resolutions*;
O'Flaherty, 'Urban politics and
municipal reform', pp 113–14, 119.

41 In 1740 the lord lieutenant
Devonshire had recommended
Massy's appointment as a justice of
the peace: letter of 23 May 1740
(Public Record Office, London, SP
63/403). For Massy serving as such
in County Clare, see: J. Frost, *The
history and topography of the county of
Clare* (Dublin 1893), p. 617.

42 J. Ingram to W. Smythe, 10 May
1744 (N.L.I., PC 445); draft letter of
W. Smythe, 18 Feb. 1743 [4]
(N.L.I., PC 449); J. Pery to W. Pery,
9 Dec. 1766 or 1767 (N.L.I., PC
875, envelope 7).

LOCAL AND NATIONAL POLITICS

1 D.W. Hayton, 'Ireland and the English
ministers'; Hayton 'The Beginnings
of the "Undertaker System"'; Hayton
'Walpole and Ireland'.

2 McNally, *Parties, patriots and undertakers.*

3 A.P.W. Malcomson, 'Speaker Pery
and the Pery papers' in *Journal of the
North Munster Antiquarian Society* 16
(1973–4), pp 49–50; C. Snoddy,
'Some notes on parliaments and its
Limerick members, 1767–1771' in
ibid. 9(1962–5), pp 170–1; J. Pery to
W. Pery, 30 Sep. [1760s] (N.L.I., PC
875, envelope 7).

4 Hayton 'Beginnings of the "Undertaker
System"'; Hayton 'Walpole and Ireland'.

5 Illuminating discussions of particular
phases of early eighteenth-century
politics include: E. Magennis, 'Politics
and administration in Ireland during
the Seven Years' War' (unpublished
Ph.D. thesis, Queen's University,
Belfast, 1996); J.G. McCoy, 'Court
ideology in mid-eighteenth century
Ireland', (unpublished M.A. thesis, St.
Patrick's College, Maynooth, 1990);
McCoy, 'Local political culture in the
Hanoverian empire: the case of
Ireland, 1714–60' (unpublished D.Phil.
thesis, University of Oxford, 1994); P.
McNally, 'The Hanoverian accession
and the Tory party'; McNally, 'Wood's
Halfpence, Carteret and the govern-
ment of Ireland, 1723–6' in *Irish
Historical Studies* xxx (1997), pp 354–76.

6 T.C. Barnard, 'New opportunities for
British settlement: Ireland 1650–1700'
in N.P. Canny (ed), *The origins of
empire*, Oxford history of the British
empire (Oxford 1998); Hayton,
'Beginnings of the "Undertaker
System"', pp 48–51.

7 J. Ingram to W. Smythe, 10 Nov.
1741, 24 Dec. 1743, 7 Jan. 1743[4]
(N.L.I., PC 445); N. Bland to Sir M.
Crosbie, 13 May 1753 (N.L.I.,
Talbot-Crosbie Mss., folder 40).

8 Copy of will of Francis Burton of Buncraggy (N.L.I., PC 563); Frost, *Clare* pp 605–6.

9 R. Purcell to Lord Perceval, 14,24 Feb. 1743[4], 2, 6, 9, 16, 27 March 1743[4], 13 April 1744, 4 Dec. 1744, 17 May 1745, 8 Oct. 1745, 5 Nov. 1745 (B.L., Additional Ms. 47001B, ff. 45, 47, 49, 51, 53v, 55, 59, 61, 95, 117, 148, 158): journal of N. Peacock, 6 & 8 March 1743[4], 24 Nov. 1745 (N.L.I., Ms. 16091): letter to J. Archdeacon, 31 Oct. 1745 (N.L.I., Ms. 827); White's annals of Limerick, (N.L.I., Ms. 2714, p. 114).

10 J. Ingram to W. Smythe, 20 July 1744 (N.L.I., PC 445).

11 Same to same, 20 Aug. 1745 (N.L.I., PC 445).

12 Connolly, *Religion, law and power*, pp 85–97; Malcomson, '"The parliamentary traffic of this country"', pp 158–61.

13 J. Kelly, *'That damn'd thing called honour': duelling in Ireland, 1570–1860* (Cork 1995); Malcomson, '"The parliamentary traffic of this country"'.

14 G.E. Howard, *A collection of apothegms and maxims for the good conduct of life* (Dublin 1767), p. 146.

15 W. Gun to Sir M. Crosbie, 14 Nov. 1751 (N.L.I., Talbot-Crosbie Mss., folder 36). In 1785 the head of the Massys descanted on 'a manliness of spirit and honour that I hope will ever be inseparable from the name'. His effusion was provoked by the prospect of *mésalliance* which would corrupt the Massys' blood. H. Massy to J. Brown, 23 Jan. 1785 (Rathkeale, Southwell-Brown Mss., box 1, bundle 5). Family honour was also invoked by Thomas Southwell in 1765. T. Southwell to J. Brown, 9 March 1765 (ibid., box 1, bundle 2).

16 M. Ward to B. Ward, 9 March 1756 (P.R.O.N.I., D 2092/1/8).

17 For the emergence of the notion of the 'protestant interest': T.C. Barnard, 'The Protestant Interest, 1641–1660' in Ohlmeyer (ed), *Ireland from independence to occupation*, pp 218–40.

18 R. Fitzgerald to Lord Brandon, 21 Feb. 1762 (Trinity College, Dublin, Ms. 3821/247).

19 A. Crookshank and D. Fitzgerald, the Knight of Glin, *The painters of Ireland, c.1660–1920* (London 1978), pp 47–9; National Gallery of Ireland, *Acquisitions 1986–88* (Dublin 1988), pp 68–71.

20 Crookshank and Fitzgerald, *Painters of Ireland*, pp 47–9.

21 Richard Beacon, *Solon: his follie* ed C. Carroll and V. Carey (Binghampton, NY 1996), pp 29–30.